INSIDER/OUTSIDER
TEAM RESEARCH

JEAN M. BARTUNEK
Boston College

MERYL REIS LOUIS
Boston University

Qualitative Research Methods
Volume 40

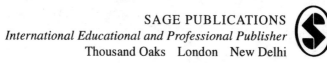

SAGE PUBLICATIONS
International Educational and Professional Publisher
Thousand Oaks   London   New Delhi

ISBN: 1356816

For information address:

SAGE Publications, Inc.
2455 Teller Road
Thousand Oaks, California 91320
E-mail: order@sagepub.com

6 Bonhill Street
London EC2A 4PU
United Kingdom

SAGE Publications, Inc.
M-32 Market
Greater Kailash I
New Delhi 110 048 India

Printed in the United States of America

Library of Congress Cataloging-in-Publication Data

Bartunek, Jean.
    Insider/outsider team research/ authors, Jean M. Bartunek and
Meryl Reis Louis.
        p. cm.—(Qualitative research methods; v. 40)
    Includes bibliographical references.
    ISBN 0-8039-7158-3 (acid-free paper).—ISBN 0-8039-7159-1 (pbk.:
    acid-free paper)
    1. Social sciences—Methodology. 2. Social sciences—Research.
I. Louis, Meryl Reis. II. Title. III. Series.
H61.B27' 1996
300'.72—dc20   96-4427

H
61
.B27
1996

96 97 98 99 10 9 8 7 6 5 4 3 2 1

This book is printed on acid-free paper.

Sage Production Editor: Gillian Dickens

CONTENTS

SERIES EDITORS' INTRODUCTION

Any social group deserving of a label is one in which members in good standing are able to distinguish insiders from outsiders. A good portion of just what allows and guides such an elementary distinction is the knowledge insiders are thought to possess, knowledge unavailable to outsiders because it rests on the shared experience, special interests, and relatively unique problems faced by members of the group. Much social research is premised on the idea that to understand a group (be it large or small, formal or informal, homogeneous or heterogeneous) requires coming to know what it is that insiders believe, value, practice, and expect. Social researchers are typically outsiders to the groups they study and thus require strategies for gaining insider understandings. Strategies in this sense are research methods such as formal and informal interviewing, participant observation, social surveys, examination of archival documents, and so on. Some of these strategies require intense interaction with insiders on their own turf over an extended period, and researchers become, for a time, insiders. Other strategies require little more than occasional visits with insiders (to collect and cart away various kinds of data), and thus researchers remain outsiders.

There is, of course, far more identity bending going on in most research studies than the above paragraph lets on. Boundaries may be permeable with much traffic in and out of the group. Borderlines between groups may overlap. Insider and outsider status may be highly relative, shifting and ambiguous. Nonetheless, method writings, although acknowledging such conditions, ordinarily direct research advice to outsiders seeking insider knowledge. This is something of a problem, because insiders also engage in social research and are certainly more than a little interested in studies that focus on their own groups. To consider insiders simply as passive respondents, subjects, informants, or specimens is to overlook many of the ways insiders shape and participate in social research. Explicit acknowledgment of the role insiders can (and perhaps should) play in the design, execution, and publication of social research comes through the formation of an insider/outsider research team.

Such teams are what interest Jean Bartunek and Meryl Louis in Volume 40 of the **Sage Series on Qualitative Research Methods**. In a manner that is both analytic and prescriptive, *Insider/Outsider Team Research* sketches out the recent growth of research partnerships and identifies many of the problems that arise across various stages of joint research projects. Several detailed examples are provided of the use of such teams. Field studies in organizational settings such as schools, community groups, and work organizations are singled out as particularly appropriate domains for insider/outsider team research, and care is taken to suggest just what is gained (and occasionally lost) as a result of such study. The authors are attentive to the disparate research goals insiders and outsiders often hold but go to some lengths to demonstrate that such differing interests may well add substantive and practical value to a project. This is not an approach suitable for all research topics; thus the limits of insider/outsider research teams are also addressed. In the end, the program advanced is a cautious one and tied closely to change or action-oriented research projects. That such work can be both scholarly and useful is a point not to be missed in this monograph.

—John Van Maanen
Peter K. Manning
Marc L. Miller

ACKNOWLEDGMENTS

We are grateful to a number of people for assistance, encouragement, and inspiration that fostered our work on this subject and the preparation of this book. We want to thank Roger Evered and Max Elden for their insights and collegiality; they should see their ideas reflected here. We thank Pennie Foster-Fishman, Christopher Keys, Catherine Lacey, and Diane Wood for their willingness to join us in extensive joint insider/outsider work and for teaching us some of what it involves. We thank Jody Diamond, Dennis Gioia, James Kelly, Mary McGann, and Molly Watt, who introduced us to joint insider/outsider efforts in a variety of disciplines. We thank Gèrard Chartrand, Barbara Davidson, Keryx Llobrera, Kristin Schulz, Jean Passavant, and Betty Pereira for high-quality research assistance and administrative support in conducting the studies and preparing this manuscript. We are grateful to Tony Athos, Linda Ducharme, Rosemary Morris, and Elizabeth Oleksak, each of whom has helped foster our personal ability to undertake our work. We are grateful to John Van Maanen for inviting us to contribute this manuscript, gently encouraging us to complete it, and working with us to enhance its readability. We thank both John and Marc Miller for thoughtful, prompt, and provocative comments on earlier drafts. Finally, we thank the Religious of the Sacred Heart and Michael Jacoby Brown for their encouragement and interest, and for serving as sounding boards and critical readers. Most of all, we thank them for providing home lives that have nourished our appreciation of what it means to live and work in relationships that span widely divergent perspectives.

INSIDER/OUTSIDER TEAM RESEARCH

JEAN M. BARTUNEK
Boston College
MERYL REIS LOUIS
Boston University

1. JOINT RESEARCH RELATIONSHIPS BETWEEN OUTSIDE RESEARCHERS AND SETTING MEMBERS

People who are insiders to a setting being studied often have a view of the setting and any findings about it quite different from that of the outside researchers who are conducting the study. These differences, we believe, have significant implications for the quality of knowledge that will be gained from the research, its potential to enhance insiders' practice, and the relationships insiders and outsiders have with each other. Consider the following examples.

Writing in the field of education, Evans, Stubbs, Frechette, Neely, and Warner (1987) criticize social science research for failing to improve educational practice. They say that the research methods typically used rely on the assumption that phenomena under study can be understood apart from the contexts in which they occur and that understandings gained by these methods apply across settings. They claim, however, that practitioners such as teachers experience events in their classrooms as affected considerably by context and do not find context-free generalizations of much use. Instead, teachers need to find immediate solutions to apparently

1

unrelated sets of everyday problems that present themselves in the classroom.

In the field of community psychology, Chesler (1991, p. 757) notes that "my associates in the Candlelighters Childhood Cancer Foundation say that much of the research on self-help is like popcorn. That is, it looks good, tastes good, it goes down easy, it takes up space, but it is not very nutritious." He goes on to comment that most research on self-help does not answer the questions of self-helpers, despite the fact that researchers care deeply about self-helpers' concerns. He suggests that perhaps this is because conventional research methods do not involve the self-help group members in the research process and do not advance group goals at the same time that they generate scholarly knowledge.

In an autobiographical essay, James Worthy (1993), who had been a director of employee relations and later a vice president at Sears, Roebuck, and Company, describes the research he conducted in collaboration with faculty members from the University of Chicago during the 1940s and 1950s. He identifies the different priorities of the practitioners and university-based researchers as exemplified by the emphasis on publishing results of the studies. He commented:

> Only small portions of Sears' research in employee relations and organizational structure were ever published. Unlike studies conducted under university auspices that typically have publication in view, studies conducted . . . by Sears . . . were basically done for administrative purposes, that is to provide officers and executives with information and recommendations helpful in the discharge of their managerial responsibilities. (p. 399)

Although these examples come from quite different fields of study and involve substantially different phenomena, each illustrates the difference in perspectives of those who are "insiders" to a particular setting—the teachers, self-helpers, and Sears' employees—and those who are "outsiders" to the setting, most often social scientists studying it. Whether the setting is a school, a community, a workplace, or some other social system, members and others who are in some way close to the setting will usually have concerns and questions about the setting, and perspectives on it, that are different from those of outside researchers.

In large part, these differences between insiders and outsiders stem from differences in their interests in gaining knowledge about the setting. Insiders need to understand their setting in order to be effective as actors and action takers. Relative to outside researchers, insiders typically see the setting under study as a source of greater and more enduring consequences in terms of economic security, social affiliation, self-esteem, challenge, and fulfillment. In contrast, outsiders typically experience the setting under study as would visitors; they are there temporarily, usually for a known period of time. Their more personally consequential settings are elsewhere. Usually, however, the outside researchers are responsible for a study of a setting. This entails framing the research, writing up results, and otherwise creating a picture of the setting for identified readers. As a result, they are likely to have much more influence over public interpretations of the settings and events in them than do insiders, the members of the setting.

In this book, we describe an approach to research in which members of settings under study work together, as co-researchers, with outsiders. In this approach, insiders and outsiders jointly examine the setting and jointly author public accounts of life in the setting. Together, they produce the sense made of the setting and knowledge to be gleaned from it. In working jointly with outsiders, insiders contribute directly to public understandings of events in the setting. We refer to this mode of inquiry as insider/outsider team research (or I/O research). In this book, we will describe the creation and use of insider/outsider team research as it occurs across various research projects.

The idea of representing insiders' perspectives in descriptions of a setting is not new. Some traditions, particularly those grounded in an interpretive paradigm and/or relying on fieldwork, have focused on capturing "the native's view" in their research efforts for 50 years or more. For example, in anthropology, ethnomusicology, fieldwork-oriented sociology, and feminist methodologies, researchers customarily have attempted to understand and make public the perspective of insiders in the setting. Sociologists trained in traditions from the University of Chicago have involved members in a wide variety of settings in studying what happens in their settings and how events there are understood (Adler & Adler, 1987). Such researchers long have noted the importance of attending to insiders' subjective meanings as fundamental in describing a setting (Gubrium, 1988). Ethnographers, by definition, have sought to understand and describe setting members' points of view (Schwartzman, 1993). Ethnomusicologists often have become custodians of aboriginal songs that help maintain cultural traditions (Ellis, 1994). Although anthropologists, ethnomusicologists, and fieldwork-oriented sociologists historically have sought to appreciate and convey insiders' experiences and perspectives, seldom have they treated insiders as co-researchers—as members of a team who together frame the questions that guide the study, gather and interpret data, and create a picture of the setting and participants' experiences in and of it. Feminist researchers have gone beyond this stance. Proponents of this more recent, emerging tradition also often undertake the mutual creation of data, in which participants in the setting under study work with outside researchers to construct the meanings that become data for later interpretation (e.g., Lather, 1988; Oleson, 1994; Reinharz, 1992).

Traditionally, researchers in many social science fields such as organizational behavior, community psychology, and education have not concerned themselves to any great extent with capturing insiders' perspectives on the setting. (There are some notable exceptions in education, including Becker [1980], Lortie [1975], Noblit [1988], Noblit and Pink [1987], and Wolcott [1973, 1990], who conduct anthropological research in educational settings.) Most researchers in these fields, more positivist than interpretive, have been oriented toward understanding the "impacts" of particular independent variables on critical dependent variables and of assessing patterns common across settings.

Recently, however, more researchers in organizational behavior, community psychology, and education (especially those focusing on teaching and teacher education) are coming to appreciate the importance of understanding research participants' perspectives. For example, Clandinin, Davies, Hogan, and Kennard (1993) described ways that they, as external educational researchers, worked with individual teachers to understand their craft and to help the teachers develop their understanding and practice of it. In community psychology, Kelly (1986, 1994) has documented the benefit of incorporating setting members' viewpoints in analyses. Organizational behavior researchers Elden and Chisholm (1993) demonstrated the value of researchers and setting members working together on various organizational investigations. As these examples illustrate, appreciation of the importance of having external researchers attend to insiders' viewpoints is growing.

As noted, even in fields with long-standing traditions of tapping insiders' perspectives, the insiders rarely join with outside researchers in studying a setting. We believe that one of the best ways to bring insiders' perspectives to a research project is to have them work as team members, as co-inquirers with outside researchers throughout the research process.

When insiders have worked with outside researchers, the focus in written reports often has been on the substantive knowledge gained from these studies (e.g., Brown, 1993; Craddock & Reid, 1993; Engelstad & Gustavsen, 1993). There is a need to focus on the methodological issues specifically involved in such joint work. Our purposes here are, first, to make the case for the efficacy of partnerships between insiders and outsiders as co-researchers, and second, to consider explicitly, and in detail, the practicalities of doing so.

In this book, we examine what it means in practice for insiders and outsiders to work together as members of a research team. We consider where and when it makes sense to employ insider/outsider research teams and when it does not, and we explore the challenges and dilemmas that arise in conducting research in this fashion. We focus particularly on the use of I/O team research in areas in which the tradition of attending to insider perspectives is not well established—particularly in education, organizational behavior, and community psychology. We draw examples from other fields and subfields with some history of including insiders' perspectives as well as leading-edge work in areas where such collaborations are now emerging.

In the remainder of this chapter, we consider what insiders bring as study team members in terms of their distinctive forms of theorizing. We conclude with brief examples from several fields to show what this mode of inquiry might look like.

Theory: Not the Sole Province of Academics

Many academic researchers, especially those from social science areas that do not have a fieldwork tradition, attempt to formulate general or "nomothetic" theories and models that apply across a broad spectrum of situations (e.g., Hermans, 1992). They design empirical studies to test hypotheses drawn from existing theories (e.g., Kahn, 1986). Theory, however, is not the sole province of academic researchers. As individuals and small groups function in their personal, social, and work lives, they are guided by their own theories. Heider (1958) referred to these as implicit theories, and Elden (1983; Elden & Levin, 1991) and others have called them local theories. Implicit or local theories are sets of heuristically developed rules of practice people use to make sense of the situations they commonly encounter, to weigh action alternatives, and to account for environmental contingencies they observe and experience. Scholarly interest in "social cognition," "cause maps," and "culture" reflects researchers' acknowledgment of the existence of local theory and their attempts to document the formation and functioning of such local theory.

There often are considerable differences between processes and characteristics of theories developed by academics and local theories (cf. Gioia, Thomas, Clark, & Chittipeddi, 1994). For example, Evans and colleagues

(1987) note that practitioners' theories concern individual cases more often than do the cross-individual generalizations developed by academics. Kelley (1992) notes that practitioners' theorizing typically addresses immediate and direct consequences of actions, time spans of minutes to days, and face-to-face interaction among small numbers of people. Elden (1983) suggests that organizational members are likely to attribute workplace problems to organizational arrangements, whereas outside researchers are more likely to attribute them to problematic people and technology.

Moreover, it is not at all evident that the theories academics produce have substantial impact on either insiders or the local theories they hold. Rather, as Barley, Meyer, and Gash (1988) demonstrate with respect to organizational culture, managers' local theories may have more impact on academics' theories than vice versa. In studying differences between academics' and managers' theories about organizational culture, Barley and colleagues note that over time, managers' understandings of this phenomenon came to have a much greater impact on the progress of academic research than did theories developed originally by academics.

Results of studies by Elden (1983), Barley et al. (1988), and Whyte (1982) suggest that not only do individuals', groups', and other setting members' local theories often have more impact on their own behavior than do researchers' more formal and general theories, but also that this is good. For example, Whyte's (1982) work demonstrated that farmers in Latin America who continued to implement their local theories about farming even after supposedly superior methods from the United States had been introduced tended to be much more successful than were farmers who adopted the new methods. This was the case in large part because the environmental conditions surrounding farming in their countries were different from the conditions surrounding farming in the United States. Thus, it is important for outside researchers to take seriously the local theories of those who participate in their studies. The examples we present below incorporate such attention and respect.

Examples of Joint
Insider/Outsider Research

In an example of I/O work drawn from community psychology (Bartunek, Foster-Fishman, & Keys, 1996), two community psychologists founded an advisory board that brought together three groups that historically had been at odds—persons with developmental disabilities, family members of persons with developmental disabilities, and professionals who work with both groups. The founders developed a model of collaborative advocacy that guided the board in its education and advocacy efforts on behalf of persons with disabilities. The model emphasizes a shared mission, the legitimacy of differences among subgroup goals, and empowering subgroups and individuals.

The founders invited an outside researcher to work with them in studying the advisory board some 2½ years after it began operating. The purpose of the study was to assess how successful the board had been in implementing the founders' collaborative advocacy model. The outside researcher observed advisory board meetings and conducted interviews with board members, and the founders collected and catalogued archival data about the advisory board's development. The outside researcher and the two founders jointly analyzed the interview data the outside researcher had collected. Results indicated that the group by and large had achieved its aims. It was externally successful, the subgroups had maintained their own individual goals, and most individual members felt "empowered."

There were differences among subgroups, however, in how they understood what empowerment meant in the advisory board. Persons with disabilities and family members tended to understand the concept of "empowerment" in much less complex terms than did the professionals. The differences in subgroup understandings of this key concept can result in conflicts among them (cf. Bartunek, Lacey, & Wood, 1992).

An example of I/O work drawn from ethnomusicology (Diamond, 1990; Diamond & Polansky, 1994) took place in Indonesia. A government policy assigns Indonesian "research counterparts" to foreign researchers so that Indonesians gain expertise by participating alongside trained scholars. As an ethnomusicologist, Diamond collaborated with I Wayan Sadra, an Indonesian composer and music critic. Working together, Diamond and Sadra commissioned and produced recordings of new works by Indonesian composers. The composers were allowed control of the recordings, and the outside researchers sought opportunities for international distribution of the recordings. Sadra, an insider, gave the outside researcher contacts, history, and insights into music and language. Diamond, an outsider, introduced Sadra to composers in other parts of Indonesia and shared with him a method for identifying Indonesian composers and their compositions. Together, they were able to select composers from different regions of the country whose work had had an impact on the evolution of experimental music. Many of the compositions selected in the project have since been broadcast in the United States and Canada.

In the field of education, a grassroots movement of teachers is emerging in which teachers join with one another and an outside researcher to study their own practice systematically. The aims of this movement are to both improve teaching practice and contribute to knowledge about teaching. This "teacher-as-researcher" mode of inquiry (Cochran-Smith & Lytle, 1993; Goswami & Stillman, 1987) has developed in opposition to conventional educational research, in which outside academics formulate knowledge and teachers are seen as transmitters, but not producers, of knowledge. In contrast, this movement fosters ways that teachers can produce knowledge based on their classroom experience.

At the heart of the teacher-researcher movement is an action research process. For example, with the help of an outside researcher-facilitator, a small group of teachers agrees to come together regularly during the school year, employing what they call a "collaborative inquiry" approach. The group agrees at the outset to present the products of joint learning to a relevant audience at the end of the year. In their meetings, individual practitioners hold up aspects of their practice to peer inspection; bring the collective resources of the group to bear on problematic aspects of the practice; and undertake, reflect on, and report back results of deliberate experiments in their practice. Formal academic publication of results may or may not be undertaken, but the group does disseminate results to other teachers (M. L. Watt, personal communication, July 14, 1995; Watt, Watt, McKiernan, & Schwartz, in press). For example, in one teacher-research group, Farmbry (1993) explored difficulties she was having as an African American teacher in a primarily African American school because she used the English language in ways different from those used by her students. On the basis of her work in the teacher-research group, she wrote a paper in which she described how she learned to use the difference between her and her students' use of the language to teach her students about complexities of using language for different audiences and to explore how ethnicity and language differences may create barriers between students and teachers.

Practitioners and researchers in the field of organizational behavior also have joined together on several occasions. Among the earliest I/O research efforts in organizational behavior were the Hawthorne studies, a joint undertaking by company researchers and university-based researchers. The studies were initiated by the Western Electric Company in 1927, and the final report of the studies was published in 1939. The studies were inspired and initiated by G. A. Pennock of Western Electric. He brought in Elton Mayo of the Harvard Business School, who with "his staff actively participated in these studies almost from their inception" (Roethlisberger &

Dickson, 1939, p. ix). Over a 12-year period, first the Western Electric researchers and then the Harvard researchers coupled a close interpretive lens with systematic observation and measurement of predefined behaviors to make sense of the effects of working conditions on the performance and morale of workers. The write-up of the history of the studies and the presentation of their cumulative findings was accomplished jointly by W. J. Dickson of Western Electric and F. J. Roethlisberger of Harvard, relative insider and outsider vis-à-vis each other and the setting.

A recent example of I/O work in organizational behavior took place at the Xerox Corporation. The study was undertaken after Xerox management proposed to "outsource" much of the work being done by union members. Peter Lazes, who had been working as a consultant for a quality of work life project at Xerox, suggested to union and management leaders that they create a "cost study team" to study possible internal changes that would save money and jobs. There were substantial risks associated with this approach for both union and management, but both sides accepted the proposal. With Lazes's facilitation, the cost study team worked extensively and creatively. It found a number of ways in which work could be done less expensively at Xerox than through outsourcing. As a consequence, a number of jobs were saved and labor leaders found new ways of working with Xerox managers. Lazes and Xerox personnel who had been involved in the change process then wrote documents, some jointly authored and some separately authored (Lazes & Costanza, 1984; Pace & Argona, 1991; Whyte, Greenwood, & Lazes, 1991), in which they described the work for practitioner and academic audiences. This research thus resulted in immediate practical outcomes and scholarly contributions to the industrial relations literature.

These examples illustrate how varied the purposes may be in I/O work. The examples from community psychology and ethnomusicology served scholarly purposes for the most part. The teacher-researcher and Xerox examples served primarily, though not exclusively, practitioner ends. Nevertheless, all the cases display a close working relationship between outside researchers and setting participants. In each, a deliberate effort was made to incorporate research participants' understandings, local theories, and knowledge about their own situations along with perspectives of the outsider researchers. Most important, some participants served as co-researchers, that is, as members of the team designing and carrying out the research.

We undertook to write this monograph in recognition of the power and propriety of this way of working. We believe that the deliberate and extensive harnessing of multiple, diverse perspectives to the task of inquiring and making sense of complex social phenomena can substantially enhance contributions to knowledge and practice. In these pages, we consider what is involved in creating and managing productive I/O research teams and what some of the dilemmas are in doing so. In Chapter 2, we put I/O work in context, tracing its intellectual roots and establishing what we mean by it. Chapter 3 breaks the research process into stages, illustrating what I/O inquiry entails at each stage. In Chapter 4, we tell an extended story of our own experience conducting two I/O studies in the same setting. Chapter 5 addresses ethical and practical considerations that arise in using I/O teams for research. In the final chapter, we highlight fundamental issues raised in doing joint I/O work and consider implications for other types of inquiry.

2. CONCEPTUAL BASES OF INSIDER/OUTSIDER TEAM RESEARCH

In June 1994, Lloyd Ryan, a Canadian educational administrator, sent an Internet message over an action research bulletin board read by people around the world interested in action research. In that message (Ryan, 1994), he presented the following illustration:

> I grew up, and still live, in a society and culture shaped by the ocean, primarily. The people live (and lived, more the latter than the former) in small isolated fishing villages along the ocean coastline, remote from urban centres, and their influences . . . .
>
> We have been subject to much scrutiny by university-based sociologists and anthropologists and folklorists, who have developed the "ideomorph" of a pristine (noble savage?) culture characterized by a "true Christian" altruistic, selfless, co-operation. As I grew to awareness of these perceptions, and to self-awareness in relation to them, I became more and more uncomfortable. It was a rather strange experience to be the subject of such scrutiny and to be aware of the nature of the scrutiny. . . . I, too, had studied at university, read sociology and anthropology . . . and, initially, was not a little amused that my culture was the subject of such interest. The discomfort derived, partially, from the fact that we . . . were being perceived in rather romanticized terms, and not without a certain indulgence concerning "our" naïveté about "the real world" which the researchers represented.
>
> Anyway, the CO-OPERATION that these Action Research people saw did not square with my ideomorphs . . . which caused me to doubt my own perceptions. I felt under considerable pressure to accept the romanticized

conception—even though I "knew" that it wasn't accurate or, at least, it didn't "square" with my perceptions of my childhood experiences and memories. (My "native tongue" was an archaic variety of English with numerous modifications, terminology additions, terminology changes, and even grammatical changes. It is spoken, now, very rarely, killed by "modern" communications!) . . . . I puzzled over the "problem."

One day . . . I overheard a resident of one village relate an incident to one of his friends from the neighboring island. Both men were relatively uneducated. (I can usually tell by the terminology utilized. They were using the "old" language.) Thus, where I (with my "education") would simply have used the term "co-operation," with its usual meanings, neither of these men would likely USE the word fluently. Consequently, these men were not "bound" by the meanings associated with that word and had to use words more closely associated with the REAL experiences and the REAL motivations.

The story concerned a family whose house had burned down and how the village had come together to build a new home for the family. (Typically, homes in these villages are not likely to be insured, in the typical fashion, both because that would require hard currency, always in rather short supply, and because insurance companies are understandably reluctant to insure homes where there is not a pressurized water supply . . .)

It was one phrase by the story-teller that played the Eureka! for me. He said "I had to do it. Next time it might be me." There it was . . . it was not co-operation in the altruistic sense. What researchers had been seeing, blinded by their concept of co-operation, was really an inter-network, consciously and deliberately developed and maintained, of obligations—an insurance scheme, in other words. That notion fitted my memories and allowed me to come to terms with the fractious and quarrelsome people who engendered and reared me in my isolated village. But more. If the family had not been "given" a house, the family would have had to move away from the island, for economic reasons. One less family would mean fewer children in the village school, fewer customers for the village merchant, fewer people overall to ensure that the next unfortunate family were cared for, less reason for the government to keep the school open . . . and less justification for keeping the nurse and clinic on the island.

Thus, it was necessary to give the family a house if the village were to survive. In other words, at root, the "selfless act of cooperation" that the researchers and the newsman saw, and as perceived by the anthropologist, was, in reality, in fact, an act of selfishness, or at least of self-preservation. Maybe the word selfishness is too strong . . . but, it explains my memories much better than the explanations of the researchers.

This is a fascinating story, one that could be discussed from multiple perspectives. We will use it to flesh out in more detail the distinction between insiders and outsiders to a setting under study. The villagers are clearly "insiders"—people carrying out the activity of helping to rebuild one another's houses. The anthropologists (and perhaps newscasters) are clearly outsiders. They show up from time to time and "explain" the behavior of the villagers.

Beyond these parties, Ryan himself is in a unique position. In relation to the anthropologists, he is an insider, having been reared in the village. In relation to the villagers, he is an outsider, having been to a university and learned the language of the outside society and of science. As a relative insider, he is aware that the outside researchers have misunderstood the villagers' motivations for their actions, but as a relative outsider, he cannot quite put his finger on the precise mistake in the researchers' misunderstandings of villagers' motivations. He no longer tacitly and fully appreciates villagers' linguistic and conceptual categories, although he understands them once they are invoked by the villagers, something beyond the grasp of the anthropologists.

The situation captured in this example of the villagers, Ryan, and the anthropologists conveys differences among the various parties in their psychological involvement and physical proximity to the setting and phenomenon under study. It also illustrates that the terms insider and outsider can be used to indicate the relation among individuals inquiring together—that is, one can speak of an actor as relatively more or less inside than another actor vis-à-vis a particular setting under study. Ryan is an outsider relative to villagers and an insider relative to other anthropologists. Finally, as we will consider in more depth later, the example points out that we are using the terms insider and outsider to capture actors' perspectives on a setting rather than merely to indicate their formal roles in those settings.

Insiders—the villagers in this example—are those individuals whose personally relevant social world is under study. As such, they do not usually engage in knowledge seeking for its own sake (cf. Van Maanen, 1988, chap. 6). Instead, through the very act of coping, a stock of local knowledge accrues to well-functioning actors that serves them as they act and is altered and refined over time in all but the most stable of social worlds. We may characterize the acquisition of local theory that emerges from their acting (Elden, 1983) as "inquiry from the inside" (Evered & Louis, 1981).

In contrast, outsiders—the anthropologists in this example—are particularly concerned with knowledge seeking for its own sake, although they may have an action orientation as well. By whatever systematic approach attends to their scientific discipline, they inquire in order to generate, test, and/or refine explanations relevant to the class of settings of which the studied setting is but one member. They seek to contribute to the stock of general knowledge (cf. Hermans, 1992) in a manner that can be characterized as "inquiry from the outside" (Evered & Louis, 1981). Their own personally relevant social worlds are not the ones presently under scientifically disciplined scrutiny. Thus, the relative primacy of action and inquiry differs between parties, as do the rules and products of inquiry employed by insiders and outsiders. Both inquire, however, and both do so in ways that address their goals.

It is this observation that leads us to suggest that by capturing, conveying, and otherwise linking the perspectives and products of inquiry of both insider and outsider, a more robust picture can be produced of any particular phenomenon and setting under study. Before proceeding to a description of how this might be accomplished, some tracing of the intellectual foundations and cognitive bases of I/O team research is warranted.

Intellectual Foundations of I/O Team Research

Although distinctions between insiders and outsiders have been drawn in sociology and other fields, different meanings have been given to them by different authors.

SOCIOLOGICAL ROOTS

Within a sociological tradition, Merton (1972) and Schutz (1964) have distinguished outsiders, as objective scientists, from insiders, as people making subjective sense of their own experience. Differences in their use of the terms are crucial to our own formulation. Schutz (1964, p. 92) contrasted insiders and outsiders in the following terms:

> Any phenomenon of the social world has a different aspect for the sociologist and for the man [*sic*] who acts and thinks within it. The sociologist . . . is the disinterested scientific onlooker of the social world. He . . . intentionally refrains from participating in the network of plans, means-and-ends relations, motives and chances, hopes and fears, which the actor within the social world uses for interpreting his experiences of it; as a scientist he tries to observe, describe, and classify the social world as clearly as possible in well-ordered terms in accordance with . . . scientific ideals. . . . The actor within the social world, however, experiences it primarily as a field of his actual and possible acts and only secondarily as an object of his thinking. . . . He organizes (his) knowledge not in terms of a scientific system but in terms of relevance to his actions.

Although subscribing to approximately the same definitions of the terms, Merton (1972) focused attention on practical implications of each standpoint and ventured into the realm of the political. He expressed concern about potential biases associated with insiders' perspectives. He described insiders as people who, because of their personal experience, sometimes understand themselves or are understood by others as having a kind of monopolistic access to particular types of knowledge. For example, people of a particular race or gender may see themselves or be seen by others as the only ones who can understand that experience. Merton argued that an approach that privileges the questions and answers of insiders is ethnocentric; it assumes that social position coincides with individual perspectives and in turn suggests (erroneously) that all insiders to a particular context think basically in the same way.

Merton further noted that social scientists sometimes have argued that outsiders are the only ones who can truly understand an insider group. In contrast, he argued that simply being an outsider does not guarantee emancipation from the myths of a collectivity. He optimistically believed, however, that training as a social scientist inculcated sufficient detachment that one could be expected to know how to assemble and assess evidence without regard to its implications for one's own group. Thus, in this sense his use of the insider/outsider distinction has political overtones.

Our own use of the distinction primarily follows that of Schutz. At the same time, we share with Merton a concern that an approach to inquiry that embraces only one perspective is potentially ethnocentric. We do not believe, however, that social science training alone prepares outside researchers to be more able than their insider counterparts to surmount their own situated perspectives.

ORGANIZATIONAL SCIENCE ROOTS

Building on Schutz's work, Evered and Louis (1981) contrasted modes of inquiry that one might employ according to the inquirer's physical and psychological distance from or connectedness to the phenomenon under study. They suggested that in "inquiry from the inside," the researcher is immersed in a setting and learns through being in the role of an actor in the real situation under study. This mode of inquiry is grounded in the epistemological assumption that knowledge comes from human experience and derives from an interpretive paradigm: By "being there," the actor comes to know. By contrast, in "inquiry from the outside," the researcher remains a detached onlooker, a nonparticipant in the social world under study. Evered and Louis likened inquiry from the outside to traditional logical positivism. The outside researcher employs a priori categories to gather factual data, meanings generated are context-free, and validation is achieved through measurement and logic. Evered and Louis further suggested that inquiry from the inside (versus inquiry from the outside) generates knowledge characterized as particular (versus universal) and idiographic (versus nomothetic), and thus was more likely to contribute to praxis or local theory than to general theory.

In 1992, Louis and Bartunek updated the Evered and Louis (1981) formulation. Rather than addressing differences in ways that insiders and outsiders working alone inquire, we focused on how insiders and outsiders might inquire jointly and how they might work together on a study. During the decade between the appearance of the Evered and Louis article and the publication of the Louis and Bartunek article, a small revolution had occurred in the organizational sciences and other social sciences not oriented toward fieldwork. Paradigmatic developments had taken place in which interpretive approaches came to be seen as legitimate alternatives and supplements to traditional logical positivist inquiry. Furthermore, by the early 1990s it was clear that outsider inquiry no longer necessarily meant purely objectivist work.

Our approach emphasizes both the connection of each researcher on the team to the setting in *absolute* terms—to what extent is a researcher an insider or an outsider?—and the connection to the setting *relative* to other members of the research team. Inside and outside researchers bring different perspectives vis-à-vis the research setting that may or may not be reflected in the formal roles they hold relative to the setting. Typically, but not always, the insider(s) will have a role as a long-term member of the setting when not involved in the study, whereas the outsider(s) will not. Typically, but not always, the outsider(s) will have a role that encompasses research activities of some type when not involved in the study, whereas the insider(s) will not. The outsider is more likely than the insider to have received formal training in social science research methods. By definition, the outsider is more detached from the research setting than is the insider. The outsider also is more concerned than the insider with uncovering generalizable knowledge; the insider is more concerned with the particular situation and with developing knowledge for direct practical use. What is the status of thinking about I/O work in other fields where it is emerging?

CURRENT FORMULATIONS
WITHIN COMMUNITY PSYCHOLOGY

Kelly (1986, 1994; Kingry-Westergaard & Kelly, 1990) has been particularly involved in what we refer to as insider/outsider team research within community psychology. He describes what he calls an ecological approach to research. By this, he means that constructs tested in research studies are developed from and by the community—the insiders themselves (cf. Kelly, 1986). As Kingry-Westergaard and Kelly note (1990, p. 29):

> Under the ecological approach, the style of work is collaborative among the participants. The process of collaborative work involves both the researchers and the other participants defining a working relationship for the integration of research and practice. . . . [It] reaffirms that research hypotheses are derived from the collaboration of the participants in the context of their working relationship. This working relationship focuses on a shared understanding of the operation of social structures, roles, and norms as they occur in given contexts. The assumed benefit of the collaborative style is that the discovery of information about the structures, roles, and norms expressed in context will enhance the authenticity, the validity, and, therefore, the usefulness of the research.
>
> The collaborative relationship becomes a social structure by which the processes of discovery and understanding can take place. The observer (researcher) and the observed (participants), in this relationship, then create together a shared agenda to discover and to understand community contexts.

CURRENT FORMULATIONS WITHIN
THE TEACHER-RESEARCHER APPROACH

The teacher-as-researcher movement involves insiders and outsiders as co-researchers. The foundations of this movement differ from those underlying the types of joint work we have described to this point. For example, Cochran-Smith and Lytle (1993) argue that apparent joint research in education is typically authored solely by university researchers, is intended for academic audiences, and makes invisible teachers' roles in the generation of knowledge about teaching and learning in classrooms. In contrast, in the teacher-researcher movement, teachers are involved in the generation of knowledge about their own activities. This movement is

> based on the notion that knowledge for teaching is "inside/outside," a juxtaposition intended to call attention to teachers as knowers and to the complex and distinctly nonlinear relationships of knowledge and teaching as they are

embedded in the contexts and the relations of power that structure the daily work of teachers and learners in both the school and the university. (Cochran-Smith & Lytle, 1993, p. xi)

In this approach, outside researchers facilitate the learning of inquiry skills by insiders and serve as resources as insiders become reflective practitioners. There is a clear expectation, contrary to Merton's view (1972), that teachers can understand their own experiences better than can outside researchers.

Cognitive Bases of Joint I/O Team Research

We have indicated conceptual foundations for the I/O approach in several disciplines, but we have yet to consider the cognitive mechanisms that enable I/O teams to make valuable research contributions. We now consider two of these mechanisms: differences in interpretive frames resulting from different experience histories and the marginal stance created by putting together these different frames.

INTERPRETIVE FRAMES AND EXPERIENCE HISTORIES

Weick (1989) makes the point quite persuasively that greater heterogeneity among conjectures or "thought trials" supports more robust theorizing. He further notes that teams of researchers are more likely to generate a greater number of diverse conjectures than are researchers working alone. We have observed and suggest to readers that research teams composed for diversity along the I/O continuum are likely to generate more diverse conjectures, or "thought trials"—to cover more interpretive as well as observational ground—than are research teams whose members are similar in their physical and psychological connections to the organizational setting under study. Along similar lines, Northcraft and Neale have observed that "successful scientific contribution results when collaborations optimize skill diversity" (1993, p. 205) and that "successful collaboration is based on a core of congruency and a healthy accompaniment of complementary dissimilarity" (p. 212).

Parties to a study come with unique experience histories, including their education, socialization, career paths, and previous involvement in the specific setting under study. In cases in which some parties are absolute insiders and some are absolute outsiders, we can expect greater diversity in the set of experience histories represented among the research team. One's experience history in turn helps shape the interpretive frames, the cognitive schemata (perspectives, in other terms) that team members bring to the tasks of perceiving, enacting, interpreting, and otherwise making sense of their worlds (Frost, Moore, Louis, Lundberg, & Martin, 1991). The more diverse the experience histories of the individuals composing a research team, especially in terms of their relationship to the setting, the more diverse should be their perspectives on and potential interpretations of any particular observed event there.

LEVERAGING RELATIVE CONNECTEDNESS
AMONG INQUIRERS INTO A MARGINAL STANCE

I/O team inquiry makes sense as well because of the ways that knowledge gains accrue to it by virtue of approximating a marginal stance. Specifically, a marginal perspective is created at the intersection of the contrasting perspectives represented by insider and outsider. Neither party need be a marginal member of her respective setting; rather, as each engages with the relative foreigner who is her partner in the venture, that party's own world is made to some extent more foreign in her own eyes. The native's usually tacit knowledge is thus made accessible through questions reflected in the outsider's questioning looks. This is not unlike the situation in which newcomers' naive questions raise to consciousness the tacit knowledge that persons experienced in a setting act on but seldom think of (Louis, 1980, 1990; Sutton & Louis, 1987).

That insiders and outsiders differ in their psychological and physical proximity to the setting studied sometimes means that the insider is straightforwardly inside the system and the outsider outside it. Other combinations also are possible. For example, Mirvis and Louis (1985) describe a researcher/consultant who had worked with a manufacturing firm periodically over an 8-year period. In this joint inquiry, the researcher/consultant enlisted the aid of a colleague in making sense of his experience and his observations of events in the firm. By design, the colleague had never set foot in the company. In this collaboration, the researcher/consultant was the (relative) insider, whereas his colleague was the (relative) outsider. The insider told the outsider the story of the firm, changes that occurred there, and his responses to events and key actors. The outsider served a clinical role, encouraging the insider to explore the relevance of his personal background and reactions to his experience in the firm. Their relative proximity to the setting—the difference in their connectedness (though neither of them was a regular member or employee of the firm)—created a marginal stance. The researcher/consultant was pulled away from his intense connectedness to the setting through his conversations with the outsider. Similarly, the outsider was made less of a stranger as the insider involved her in looking at his experience. Together, their temporarily altered perspectives approximated the experience of being marginal, without leaving either party at the margin in the long term. This illustration also suggests the wide divergence in what is meant by relative connectedness to a setting.

Action Orientation Within I/O Research

Some I/O research teams are concerned primarily with producing contributions to scientific knowledge. Other teams are concerned primarily with informing and enhancing practice in the setting under study. Concern with taking action is fundamental to the use of I/O teams in the action research tradition.

Since its inception in the 1940s (Collier, 1945; Lewin, 1946), action research has referred to the use of scientific approaches to study important organizational or social problems in concert with the people who experience these problems (Rapoport, 1970). Efforts are designed to produce new knowledge that contributes both to practical solutions to immediate problems and to general knowledge (Elden & Chisholm, 1993).

In recent years, several variants of action research have emerged, including participatory action research (PAR) (Whyte, 1991), participatory research (Park, Brydon-Miller, Hall, & Jackson, 1993), action science (Argyris, Putnam, & Smith, 1985), and action inquiry (Torbert, 1991). Because both PAR and participatory research have been used in a variety of social science disciplines, we will provide examples of them in this book. Both emphasize practical contributions prior to scholarly ends and involve research participants in inquiry about their settings. They differ in attention to political issues.

PAR has been described by Deshler and Ewert (1995) as a process of systematic inquiry in which those experiencing a problematic situation in a community or workplace participate jointly with trained researchers in deciding the focus of knowledge generation, in collecting and analyzing information, and in taking action to manage, improve, or solve their problem situation. The Lazes and Costanza (1984) study is an example of this type of approach, as are Levin's (1993) use of PAR to create social networks that support regional economic development in Norway and Engelstad and Gustavsen's (1993) use of networks to implement a nationwide PAR-based Swedish reform effort.

In contrast, Deshler and Ewert (1995) described participatory research as a process of combining education, research, and collective action on the part of oppressed groups working with popular educators and community organizers. The knowledge that is generated is intended to help solve practical problems within a community and, ultimately, contribute to a fairer and more just society. Its primary purpose is to encourage the poor and oppressed and those who work with them to generate and control their own knowledge. . . . This tradition emphasizes full and active participation of powerless people, and a stress on ideological, political, and economic dimensions.

Speaking from the perspective of participatory research, Cancian and Armstead (1992, p. 1429) comment that PAR gives "little attention to power and empowerment, or consciousness raising and education, and the action component of the projects is coordinated with management and does not directly challenge the existing power structure. However, we believe such issues are central to participatory research." Examples of participatory research projects include an organizational intervention aimed at helping farmers in India deal with problems in their villages (Brown, 1985) and an educational intervention aimed at assisting developmentally disabled adults with the creation of musical theater productions (Lynd, 1992).

As these varied research traditions indicate, I/O team research can take a number of orientations. These may range in the extreme from purely scholarly aims to an exclusive action focus on behalf of the poor and oppressed. When we say that outside researchers and insider participants work together throughout the research process, what the "throughout" means in practice depends in part on the orientation of the research.

Characteristics of I/O Team Research

From this look at the foundations of I/O team research, we can identify several distinguishing features of this mode of inquiry. A research effort constitutes an example of I/O teamwork to the extent that

1. a research team is responsible for the study;
2. the research team is composed of people who differ in their physical and psychological connectedness to the research setting and focal questions being examined;
3. insider members of the research team contribute beyond serving merely as sources of data—they work jointly with the outside researcher in designing the research, collection, and analysis of data; interpreting results; and crafting the story presented about the setting; and

4. insider and outsider members of the team share authority for decisions about the content of the story told about the phenomena/setting under study.

Although enhanced practice or systems change is not formally included as a defining characteristic of I/O work, it is a feature of many forms of joint work such as action research and its variants. Even when the primary focus is scholarly, some practical effects on insiders can be expected as by-products of joint I/O inquiry within a setting.

As we noted earlier, although some social science disciplines have a tradition of capturing participants' perspectives, these approaches traditionally have not focused on involving insiders throughout the various stages of a research project. Joint work throughout the stages of research distinguishes I/O research from, for example, much ethnographic work. In most participant observation and ethnographic studies, researchers make use of key informants or guides. Typically, informants are there to respond to researchers' requests but do not act as co-researchers; that is, informants do not see early drafts, let alone participate in writing them. In contrast, when I/O teams are used, the involvement of both insiders and outsiders is at least consultative, and often highly participative, throughout the project.

3. CONDUCTING JOINT
INSIDER/OUTSIDER RESEARCH

In *The Cornell Chronicle,* an in-house publication of Cornell University, Costello (1994) recently published an article on the work on William Foote Whyte. The article refers in part to the best-selling monograph in the history of sociology, Whyte's *Street Corner Society,* a book about the North End of Boston in the 1930s. The article provides a glimpse into aspects of the study relevant to insider/outsider team research.

In 1936 . . . William Foote Whyte began working in the slum district of the North End of Boston. . . . "When I began the project in Boston, the goal of my research was to understand the social structure and patterns in relation to the economic problems of a depressed urban area," Whyte explained. But as he began working with gang leader Ernest Pecci, who served as Whyte's key contact and informant, Whyte found himself discussing his work and ideas with Pecci. . . . At Pecci's suggestion, Whyte . . . took on an assistant, Angelo

Ralph Orlandella. "I was able to get $100 from Harvard for this high school drop-out to serve as my research assistant," Whyte recalls. "I had long discussions with Ralph . . . about the problems of the North End; the fact that they had one stony dirt playground and very poor living conditions." Together Whyte and Orlandella organized a march on City Hall that got the attention of the media and politicians and produced immediate results for the dilapidated neighborhood.

This excerpt illustrates two points about the conduct of insider/outsider research on which we will focus in this chapter. First, insiders living and/or working within a particular setting may have a great deal to contribute to the intellectual understanding of the setting, even though they may not be trained in social science methodology. Second, activities that arise during I/O research may serve both scholarly and practical ends. Carrying out scholarly research does not necessarily preclude having members of the research team involved in activities of practical significance to setting members. Conversely, carrying out activities imbued with practical relevance does not necessarily preclude insider and outsider researchers from making a scholarly contribution.

In this chapter, we turn to the practicalities of doing research from an I/O perspective. Our guiding question is this: What is entailed in carrying out insider/outsider team research? As we saw in Chapter 2, gains accrue in I/O work as multiple, highly contrasting viewpoints are brought to bear and maintained in tension. When one viewpoint is given voice only at the discretion of another, when mutual influence is compromised or is mere artifice, potential gains (scholarly and practical) will be compromised as well. The operative feature is a genuine joint influence of insider and outsider research team members throughout the cycle of research. Our purpose here is to examine what joint influence means and what it looks like at each stage in a research effort. We consider ten stages:

- Composing the I/O research team
- Developing a working relationship between insiders and outsiders
- Formulating research questions to orient the study
- Designing data collection processes
- Collecting data
- Analyzing and interpreting data
- Writing reports and presenting results
- Taking action in the setting

- Making scholarly contributions
- Tracking outcomes of the collaboration

Before beginning a discussion of the specific stages, we need to put in perspective the notion of stages and how we will talk about them. For the sake of discussion, we will discuss activities and events associated with conducting joint I/O work as if they occurred in chronological sequence and as discrete stages. It is rarely the case, however, especially in qualitative research, that stages proceed in discrete steps or in the exact sequence presented. For example, activities begun at certain stages, such as developing the working relationship between insiders and outsiders, may continue throughout the research effort. Formulation of specific research questions may occur after or as initial data are collected and examined. In some modes of inquiry, such as PAR or participatory research, action taking is pervasive throughout the project.

The particular characterizations of stages of research we present are crafted to depict the vocabulary of research common in organizational behavior, educational research, and community psychology, fields on which we focus in this book. These are disciplines not steeped historically in a tradition of attending to insiders' perspectives or relying on field-based approaches to inquiry. Had we focused on explicating insider/outsider team research in the context of a fieldwork tradition, we might have written this chapter quite differently. Readers with a field research perspective are asked to take these matters into account.

We do not present a set of rules for practice based on our experience or reading of what others have done. Rather, we highlight issues that crop up in various types of accounts of I/O work and provide examples from actual studies to illustrate the many ways an issue has been handled in practice. The studies we present, some of which use only partial I/O approaches, were chosen to illustrate some of the many ways insiders and outsiders might work together in research at different stages of a project. We use these studies here solely to illustrate the different approaches vis-à-vis I/O work. We are not holding them up as exemplary in all respects. In our view, a mode of exposition that uses multiple examples reflects the natural complexities and contingencies inherent in any research endeavor, the extent and limits of our expertise, and the spirit of mutuality inherent in I/O work.

As we discuss joint I/O work, we are not necessarily advocating *equal participation* among insider and outsider researchers at each stage in the project. Sometimes—and for very good reasons—the parties agree that one should be more involved than the other at some particular stage. What is important is that decisions about the relative participation of the parties at various stages in the project reflect a process of mutual consultation and discussion. In this way, both insiders and outsiders have influence throughout the study. An overview of ways that issues attendant to joint I/O work at each stage may be handled is shown in Table 3.1.

Stage I: Composing the I/O Research Team

What becomes joint I/O inquiry may or may not start out as such. Sometimes research is conceived from the outset as joint work; in other cases, the joint work emerges. An outside researcher may be spending time in a setting and in so doing may come to recognize the desirability and feasibility of working jointly with inside research partners, or research may be initiated by insiders who recognize the desirability of working with outside researchers. Regardless of who instigates the joint work, one of the first considerations in implementing this approach typically has to do with composing the research team, either through outsiders selecting insiders or insiders selecting outsiders.

OUTSIDERS SELECTING INSIDERS

We deal first with what is probably the more typical experience: outside researchers selecting insider members of the research team. When outsiders initiate the research, they must decide who composes the potential "population" of insiders with whom they might work. As Clark and Moss (1995) note, this depends in part on the form of joint I/O research. In most I/O approaches, including scholarly work, action research, or PAR, any or all setting members are potential insider researchers. In contrast, in projects conducted in a participatory research mode, researchers would seek out as insider research partners members of groups they or the group members themselves consider to be oppressed. They would do this in lieu of seeking mutual influence with members of dominant groups whose influence, according to this perspective, has been overrepresented in past inquiry and reform efforts (cf. Brown & Tandon, 1983).

In general, it is important for outside researchers to choose at least some insiders who have wide access across the aspects of the setting that are pertinent to the research or are powerful enough within the setting to provide the team with fairly full access. (In the case of participatory research, less powerful insiders will not have this access.) In addition,

TABLE 3.1 Summary of Insider/Outsider Research Stages

Stages	*Key Issues*
I. Composing the I/O research team	Those who initiate the research choose insider or outsider partners. Criteria for choosing insiders include wide access in the setting, interest in the research, and ability to appreciate others' perspectives. Criteria for choosing outsiders include trust, ability to work jointly, and research skill.
II. Developing a working relationship	Mutual respect and influence are essential in the development of the working relationship. The research addresses the goals of both parties.
III. Formulating research questions to orient the study	Insider and outsider researchers develop questions to orient the study. Together, they may decide on a common set of questions. One group may have more say than the other, or they may have equal say in this decision.
IV. Designing data collection processes	Insider and outsider researchers design the data collection process. Insiders may give an external researcher guidance in methods and specific questions to be addressed, or the groups may jointly design these.
V. Collecting data	Insiders and outsiders may collect the same types of data or complementary data. Insiders, with guidance from outsiders, may collect the data. Outsiders may collect the data.
VI. Analyzing and interpreting data	Insiders and outsiders may analyze the data together. One party may provide a tentative interpretation, and the other may critique and advance the interpretation.
VII. Writing reports and presenting results	One party may write the report and obtain comments on drafts from the other party. Insiders and outsiders may author the report jointly, or parties may write separate papers.
VIII. Taking action	Action is undertaken based on the research and aimed at benefiting setting participants.
IX. Making scholarly contributions	The research makes a contribution to scholarly literature in some area.
X. Tracking outcomes	Researchers assess the extent to which project goals were achieved.

insiders chosen must have an interest in being involved in the research and in understanding the setting from the eyes of other setting members, even if others' understandings and values do not correspond to their own perspectives. It helps if insiders have some social science research training, but, as we will illustrate below, relatively less trained groups can collect and analyze data from their own setting quite effectively if they receive appropriate guidance from an outside researcher.

Jean Bartunek often has had as her co-researchers people who were instrumental in founding the setting being studied (e.g., Bartunek et al., 1992; Bartunek et al., 1996). This is a kind of "natural selection" process that typically is accepted by other setting members. When the outside researcher is working with setting leaders or founders, however, he or she needs to develop relationships with other setting members as well or risk others' suspicions of being an agent or advocate for the leaders or founders. The outside researcher might, for example, take steps to be seen as someone to whom other setting members can talk *about* the leaders, even if it is known that the leaders eventually will hear the information.

In many studies, the outside researcher does not know particular setting members at the outset of a study, and so needs to find ways to contact potential inside members and engage them in the research. There are several ways of doing this. Farrell, for example (Farrell, 1994; Farrell, Peguero, Lindsey, & White, 1988), has in two separate studies engaged low-income high school students in collecting data from and about other low-income students. One of the studies dealt with low-income students at risk of dropping out of high school. Farrell met students in danger of dropping out of high school at a college program established specifically to work with such students and recruited his co-researchers from this population based on recommendations from teachers and others associated with the program.

Whitmore (1994) was an outside researcher commissioned by a granting agency to evaluate a prenatal education program for single, expectant mothers, many of whom received social assistance as their primary source of income and many of whom had relatively low educational levels. The granting agency was sensitive to the fact that many of the women participating in the program had limited reading and writing skills and would find responding to a traditional questionnaire threatening. Whitmore suggested a research approach in which she would hire a group of program participants as coevaluators and train them to do the evaluation with her. The granting agency accepted this proposal. Whitmore drafted a letter to all participants in the prenatal program for the past 3 years inviting them to apply to be co-researchers. She included an application form requesting basic information, a reference, and a brief statement of interest. The letter was followed up by a program staff member who encouraged the women to apply. All six who applied were interviewed to determine characteristics such as reliability and probable comfort in talking with strangers. The final choice of the four-member research team was based on these interviews.

INSIDERS SELECTING OUTSIDERS

Sometimes insiders select outsiders to work with them. Important criteria for this selection process include the outside researcher being able to work jointly with insiders and being skilled in the type of research to be undertaken. In PAR or participatory research projects, insiders often select outsiders such as consultants who already have been part of the setting and have proven themselves trustworthy and skilled (Whyte et al., 1991). They might select an outsider institution based on its reputation of working in ways consistent with what insiders are trying to accomplish. This is illustrated in a participatory research project that involved residents of North Bonneville, Washington, as insiders, with students and faculty at Evergreen State College acting as outside researchers (Comstock & Fox, 1993). The residents of North Bonneville were facing eviction and relocation as a result of a decision by the U.S. Army Corps of Engineers to build a powerhouse on a dam located in the center of their town. The residents appealed to the college for help in relocating as a community, rather than as dispersed individuals and families. They did this in part because of the college's publicized alternative curricular structure that enabled students and faculty to pursue problems or issues, such as the structure and function of communities, and the experience that Russell Fox, one of the professors there, had in other participatory research projects.

Whether the primary purpose of the research is action or scholarly, trust, the capacity to work together, and research skill are important to insiders selecting outsiders. For example, Robert Krim, the founder of the Boston Management Consortium, invited Jean Bartunek to work with him in studying and writing about the work of the consortium (Humphries, Krim, & Bartunek, 1995). This invitation was based, in part, on the fact that Krim and Bartunek had known each other in other contexts and trusted each other. Krim knew that Bartunek was familiar with the work of the consortium and that her scholarly writing was potentially consistent with the type of writing he hoped to do as the research proceeded.

Stage II: Developing a Working Relationship

Developing successful working relationships among I/O team members may be difficult because of the differences in experience, perspective, and interests between insiders and outsiders. The greater the differences between insiders and outsiders (e.g., in background and images of research processes), the greater the challenge the two parties face in building a working relationship.

The typical relationship between insider and outsider members of a research team is characterized more by contrasts than by similarities. It is in many respects intercultural. As Van Maanen notes, "The crucial problem of what we so cavalierly call 'writing it up' is to balance, harmonize, mediate, or otherwise negotiate a tale of two cultures (the fieldworkers' and the others')" (1988, p. 138). Guidelines for building any intercultural relationship apply, including recognizing potential differences in the language, meanings, and consequences associated with events, actions, and communications in the eyes of different team members (Hall, 1981).

Necessary for successful joint work by insiders and outsiders is the development of mutual respect, honesty, and trust (Diamond, 1990; Ellis, 1994; Lampton & Tunstill, 1994; Northcraft & Neale, 1993). It is particularly important that outside researchers demonstrate respect for the culture and traditions of the insiders. When the research project involves something sacred to the insiders, as is the case with much anthropological and ethnomusicological research, reverence in addition to respect is warranted. It also is important to establish norms that show evidence of valuing the diverse perspectives and differentiated ways that insiders and outsiders can contribute to research (Kelly, Azelton, Burzette, & Mock, 1994). Useful processes for accomplishing this in diverse groups (such as I/O research teams) include facilitating extensive face-to-face contact among the parties, enabling them to practice social skills that facilitate cooperation and individual accountability where the individual contribution is explicit, finding means for fostering good communication between members, and reinforcing the acquisition and use of adequate conflict management skills (Dyer, 1987; Kelly et al., 1994). In addition, when either the insider or outsider role is fulfilled by a group rather than by individuals, difficulties may arise that are associated with the dispersion of responsibility and accountability, sense of ownership, authority, and voice. Awareness of potential difficulties and explicit discussion of such issues among research participants are important to the development of a well-functioning research team.

Although it is important to address explicitly the aims of both insiders and outsiders, there may be clashes between these aims. In ethnomusicology, for example, an aim for aboriginal peoples may be ensuring that only those who have been initiated properly into a particular group hear particular kinds of music, whereas the aims of outside researchers include making traditional music more widely available to external audiences (Lampton & Tunstill, 1994).

A more or less formal contract can address and incorporate means of managing clashes in aims. Such a contract can be established at the beginning of the research process and reviewed or revised during it. Whether the contract is oral or written, it is useful to the parties in acknowledging one another's concerns, aims, and contributions. Comstock and Fox (1993) illustrated such a contracting process in the North Bonneville project. College personnel agreed to work with town members. They began by preparing a written proposal for a multistage project that would involve joint work by college personnel and residents. The proposal was discussed at a town meeting, allowing everyone the opportunity to participate in the decision to pursue the project and the resulting research. This provided a comfortable foundation for their later joint work.

In discussing and contracting about ways each party will contribute to the venture, bases for effective collaboration include building on the distinctive competence and perspective of each team member while providing opportunities for members to develop new skills. It is important to be explicit about how the research team will make decisions, communicate among team members, and handle differences. Team members' comfort in raising different views and risking conflict, and therefore their willingness to do so, increases as a function of their confidence in the team's ability to deal with differences. Having candid conversations up front about how to address these issues can pay off in terms of reflecting multiple perspectives.

Beyond initial conversations about norms, an effective I/O team will build in ways of monitoring how it is doing and how members feel about the research process and their contribution to it. The ways this might take place include periodic "time out" sessions for process debriefing among team members, trading off responsibility for attending to group process issues within the team during joint work sessions, and up-front contracting to legitimize calling for time outs when issues warranting attention arise during the research.

Stage III: Formulating Research
Questions to Orient the Study

The formulation of specific questions to orient the research effort generally comes early in a research project. In much traditional social science research, an outside researcher determines the guiding questions or hypotheses. Often, participants in a study do not know the true focus of the study. In contrast, in I/O teams insider and outsider researchers together influence the framing of the research questions.

The study of the disabilities advocacy group referred to in Chapter 1 (Bartunek et al., 1996) illustrates a situation in which insiders and outsiders together determined the particular research questions. A study by Pasmore and Friedlander (1982) illustrates a situation in which researchers enabled the participants to specify the hypotheses pursued within a domain of common interest. In this case, two university-based researchers conducted an action research project at an electronics manufacturing facility in which employees were experiencing repeated injury problems. Rather than formulating hypotheses about the injury problems themselves, Pasmore and Friedlander brought together a representative group of employees at the plant and had them talk about possible reasons for the injuries. The employees generated a list of hunches about the causes of the injuries, and these hunches served as the basis for the research. Similarly, in the study of North Bonneville, the residents had primary say over the issues they wanted researched regarding the relocation of their community, especially in terms of what procedures would be available to them for influencing the decision of the Army Corps of Engineers.

Stage IV: Designing Data Collection Processes

The next task is selecting specific methods for collecting data, such as the interview, observational, or questionnaire schedules to be used. Insiders may participate fully in this activity, may provide general guidance as to how to address specific questions in which they are interested, and/or may react to an outsider's proposals for data collection. Sometimes insiders are better at designing specific questions to be asked, and ways of asking them, in a particular setting than are outside researchers who are less familiar with the research setting. Sometimes the issue is one of determining what will constitute data in the study.

The study by Whitmore (1994) illustrates a situation in which the basic research guidelines were created externally but insiders and outsiders together determined the data collection procedures. The primary purpose of the research was to determine the effectiveness of the prenatal program. This was established at the outset by the granting agency. The coevaluators worked together to design the data collection process, including designing the specific interview questions and interview formats for program participants and a mailed survey to professionals in the community who had contact with the program participants.

The Whitmore example illustrates a situation in which insiders were involved in the design of the data gathering tools. There are other illustrations of this. For example, in the disabilities advocacy study, all three researchers participated in designing the interview protocols used to pursue research objectives. At the manufacturing facility studied by Pasmore and Friedlander (1982), the employees' hunches about the causes of injuries formed the basis of questions designed by the outside researchers that were asked of plant personnel in interviews and surveys.

Other ways are available for insiders to provide important information to outside researchers in the design of data collection procedures. An expectation underlying many studies of quality of working life (QWL) interventions has been that some participants in the companies implementing the QWL interventions—specifically members of the labor-management committees—contribute to the design of questionnaires aimed at assessing the success of the intervention. For example, Israel, Schurman, and Hugentobler (1992) conducted an action research project focused on sources of occupational stress in collaboration with a QWL committee in a manufacturing plant. They involved members of a joint labor-management committee in the design of a survey instrument that was administered to all employees in the plant.

Sometimes it is difficult to integrate insiders' preferences and wisdom concerning modes of collecting data. For example, Kelly (1993) described a study of African American leaders in the Chicago area, carried out with the advice of a research panel composed of members of the local African American community. The panel's purpose was to advise the outside researchers on means of documenting the development of community leaders. The outside researchers found it challenging to integrate the panel's views with their own psychological research traditions. For example, the panel believed that data collection required having leaders tell their own stories. In psychological research, however, interviewees customarily respond to structured questions rather than telling their own stories in a more open-ended format. In response to suggestions from the panel, the research team designed a data collection procedure in which respondents began by telling their stories and the interviewer followed up with more structured questions linked to the respondents' stories.

Stage V: Collecting Data

Insiders working with outsiders can be involved in data collection in a variety of ways. For example, in Pasmore and Friedlander's (1982) action research study of illness at a manufacturing plant, outside researchers and insider employees worked together in conducting interviews and administering surveys at the plant.

Clandinin's (1989) study illustrates a situation in which an insider and an outsider collected complementary data. Clandinin worked with a novice teacher to explore the development of the teacher's personal, practical knowledge during his first year of teaching. The teacher kept a daily journal in which he recorded significant classroom experiences and gave it to the outside researcher on a weekly basis. During the year, the teacher met with the outside researcher for several informal conversations and to conduct three semistructured interviews in which they discussed the teacher's journals and reflections on this experience. The outside researcher tape-recorded each interview and sent a copy of the interview transcript to the teacher prior to the next interview.

Another type of complementarity occurred in the developmental disabilities advocacy study (Bartunek et al., 1996). As noted earlier, the insider researchers collected archival data about the setting. Although the insiders and outsider together designed interview questions, the outside researcher alone conducted interviews with the other board members. This division of labor enabled other board members to talk candidly about sensitive issues while maintaining confidentiality.

Sometimes insiders alone collect the data. Farrell, for example, in his studies of low-income high school students, trained his student co-researchers to conduct relatively unstructured interviews. The student co-researchers then conducted and taped interviews with their peers and, when appropriate, with their teachers.

In the Whitmore (1994) evaluation of the prenatal program, the women who were program participant/insider researchers conducted the interviews of other program participants. In addition, Whitmore and her insider partners met weekly during the data collection period, sharing their experiences and preliminary impressions.

Participatory researcher Merrifield (1993) engaged insiders in a less traditional form of data collection in a project aimed at helping residents in Kingsport, Tennessee, deal with environmental health problems in their community. Despite official denials, residents of Kingsport were convinced that toxic wastes were being dumped in their town and that this accounted for the abnormally high incidence of health problems they were experiencing. Kingsport residents found it difficult to get adequate information about the chemicals because none of them had sufficient knowledge or education to penetrate the technical language used by corporate and government officials. Because one aim of the participatory research project was to help the residents gain access to information about problems that affected them, the outside researchers conducted a workshop in which people in areas experiencing hazardous waste problems came together to discuss their problem. At the workshop, the residents of Kingsport discovered that they were not alone in their concerns. Following the workshop, some participants traveled to the offices of the state department of public health to obtain documents about chemicals buried in their landfills, an important form of data gathering. They compiled a list of the chemicals and then resorted to a combination of medical, chemical, and Webster's dictionaries to gain information on the potential health effects of those chemicals and to translate this information into language they could understand. What came out of the exercise was a list of chemicals suspected to have been dumped in their neighborhoods, along with their potential health effects. In such a fashion, residents began to believe that they had some control over the information.

Stage VI: Analyzing and Interpreting Data

A distinct advantage of I/O team research is that an array of interpretive lenses and experience histories is brought to bear when identifying, analyzing, and interpreting patterns observed in the data. The process of working together on these tasks may take different forms. One partner may develop a draft interpretation that is critiqued and reinterpreted by the other partner. For example, in the QWL study conducted by Israel and her colleagues (1992), outside researchers analyzed the quantitative data generated through questionnaires the insiders helped to design. Insider labor-management committee members then used the survey results to identify sources of stress in the plant. Together, they developed interventions aimed at reducing the sources of stress.

In the narrative inquiry approach of Connelly and Clandinin (1990; Clandinin & Connelly, 1994), the outside researcher's interpretation of data is critiqued and advanced by the inside researcher. For example, in the study of the development of the novice teacher's personal and practical knowledge, Clandinin, as the outside researcher, drafted a narrative description of the teacher's experience based on the data they had collected and shared it with the teacher in the form of a long letter. The letter included the outsider's description of the teacher's classroom activities and tentative interpretations. The teacher then responded, modifying the outside researcher's account so that the final report was based on the interpretations of both parties. This method provided the teacher with considerable opportunity to influence the outside researcher's understanding of events.

Joint data analysis is represented in the disabilities advocacy study by Bartunek and her colleagues. Here, as noted, inside and outside research partners jointly designed the interview schedule. The outside researcher was the one to collect data, on the basis of this schedule, because of the sensitive nature of the issues covered in the interview. After interview responses were transcribed and the outside researcher had coded the data to ensure anonymity of the interviewees, all three researchers analyzed the data. Working in pairs, they content analyzed the major themes expressed in interview responses, isolating differences in the pattern of themes used by different subgroups in the setting.

Farrell (Farrell, 1994; Farrell et al., 1988) describes ways that he and his high school student co-researchers jointly analyzed the interview data the high school students collected. Taped interviews of "at-risk" students and of "highly successful" students were transcribed. Farrell trained his co-researchers to identify themes present in the data. He provided each of them with copies of each interview transcript. Student research partners underlined, on their own copies, the most telling comments made by those interviewed. Comments underlined by all the students were considered the most crucial, and analysis focused on them.

In the evaluation of the prenatal program, Whitmore (1994) and the women she worked with cut up copies of the transcripts of the interviews each had conducted and put the answers to each of the interview questions in separate envelopes. They then divided up the envelopes, content analyzed the responses, and developed preliminary category schemes. Each person presented her own analyses to each of the others, after which the group discussed the interpretations offered. This process went on until they reached a common understanding of meanings.

Participatory research also involves insiders in data analysis. In the North Bonneville case, as the residents talked with students about their community and the importance of maintaining it, they became even more disturbed about the Army Corps of Engineers' plan to relocate individual families to different areas. This awareness led town members to seek to exercise more control in their own situation, strengthening their resolve to press for communal relocation.

Stage VII: Writing Reports and Presenting Results

In I/O team research, insiders and outsiders work together to prepare the story that will be told to other practitioners and/or scholarly audiences. Historically, producing a published report has been more salient in scholarly oriented projects than in action-oriented projects, whereas presentation of practical implications of results has predominated in action-oriented projects.

In the study of occupational stressors by Israel and her colleagues (1992), the outside researchers gave successive drafts of the report to the QWL committee members, whose comments and recommendations were incorporated into revisions. In the prenatal evaluation study (Whitmore, 1994), the research partners worked together to identify the main points to be made in the final report. Whitmore then drafted the report, and others made modifications to it. All members of the research team participated in oral presentations of results of the work to a women's research conference at a local university. In Clandinin's narrative inquiry approach, the outside researcher typically works with the teacher to draft a narrative account of the teacher's classroom practice. The outside researcher and teacher then rework the draft, mutually constructing the story of the events that occurred. Final versions of the account are then "validated" by the teacher (Clandinin, 1989; Connelly & Clandinin, 1990).

Joint authorship represents a second approach to writing reports in I/O collaborative work. In the disabilities advocacy study, the outside researcher and the two inside researchers individually authored different parts of the initial draft. The insiders prepared a description of their model, knowledge gained from archival materials, and portions of the interview results. The outsider prepared the introduction, the methods and discussion sections, and part of the results section. The classic management studies of Roethlisberger and Dickson (1939), Coch and French (1948), and Trist and Bamforth (1951) represent other instances of joint authorship by insider and outsider members of a research team.

Levin (1993) described the use of joint authorship in a participatory action research effort in Norway to create social networks to support regional economic development. Outside action researchers created search conferences involving participants who represented multiple constituencies in a local area. The outside action researchers then worked together with the search conference participants in preparing a report for local governments that summarized and communicated the outcomes of the search conferences. They found that writing the document legitimized the development process for themselves and extended the knowledge produced to nonparticipants.

Outside researchers and insiders may author separate papers about events in which they participated jointly. In Whyte's (1991) edited book on participatory action research, for example, Whyte and colleagues wrote a chapter describing their participative action research work at Xerox and at a worker cooperative in Mondragon, Spain. Insiders with whom they had worked wrote their own, separate, chapters (e.g., Pace & Argona, 1991; Costanza, 1991), in which they often presented somewhat different views of the same work.

Finally, insiders may write their own reports. This is particularly likely in the teacher-researcher movement. Many books published from this movement (e.g., Cochran-Smith & Lytle, 1993; Watt, in press) contain chapters by teachers that describe the outcomes of the work they conducted in their teacher-research groups. The papers by Farmbry (1993) and Watt and colleagues (in press) introduced earlier are two examples of this type of work.

Stage VIII: Taking Action

One product of participatory research, action research, and PAR is some type of action taken that improves the lot of the insiders participating in the study. In I/O studies that have more of an action orientation, a scholarly contribution is sometimes a less important outcome of the inquiry effort.

In the PAR study at Xerox described in Chapter 1, the effort was directed at saving jobs. From this perspective, the joint research was a success in that jobs were saved. Other changes included the inclusion of workers as participants in future job redesign efforts, considerable cost savings for the company, and the establishment of similar worker participation groups in other Xerox locations.

Other illustrations of action outcomes are seen in the two participatory research projects discussed earlier in this chapter. One outcome of the participatory research project on environmental health problems in Tennessee was increased knowledge and a sense of control among members of the community. Training in environmental and occupational health for community participants has continued, and lead investigator Merrifield has found that the likelihood of success in programs of this sort is increased when insider partners recognize a strong personal incentive to take action in response to events that affect them.

In the case of North Bonneville, students working with the residents published a lengthy planning study summarizing what they and the townspeople had come to understand about the community. The next year, the college students and townspeople formed a planning commission that trained volunteers to conduct a comprehensive relocation preference survey in which most of the townspeople (including children) participated. The town council found a site for the new town. The town drafted the plan, and the Washington State congressional delegation passed into law a statute obligating the Army Corps of Engineers to pay for a town site and detailed planning. Three years later, the new city was officially dedicated. The new town appears to reflect residents' preferences better than did the old town site.

Stage IX: Making Scholarly Contributions

Some I/O work results in contributions of a scholarly nature that add value beyond the knowledge gained about the particular setting under study and beyond guides for action for participants in this or similar settings. Scholarly contributions occur when, in writing and/or through presentations, the I/O research team advances theoretical understandings of phenomena of relevance beyond the setting studied.

For example, in the disabilities advocacy study, the researchers crafted and assessed an original conceptual model of intergroup relationships that describes conditions under which groups that differ in status, power, and ability can work together in a way that is productive and "empowering" for all the members. This model contributes to the body of empirical and conceptual literature on intergroup relationships in social settings.

In another example, Farrell and his colleagues (1988) went beyond much educational research in studying the perceptions and experiences of high school students at risk. Results of this study indicated that these students often experience pressure and boredom as central features of their lives, and that boredom and pressure interfere with the development of their sense of identity. Thus, this study brought a phenomenological foundation to existing knowledge about students at risk.

Finally, as we noted earlier, action research projects sometimes have a scholarly component. For example, the Pasmore and Friedlander (1982) study of accidents in a manufacturing plant resulted in the development of a conceptual model applicable beyond that setting. The model captures ways in which work designs, in combination with workforce characteristics such as conscientiousness, contribute to the production and/or management of stress and illness at work. This study makes an empirically based contribution to the body of knowledge about workplace stress.

Not all I/O team research results in such scholarly contributions. The possibility of this type of contribution, however, might well be kept in mind as teams are composed, project aims are set, results are assessed, and plans for their dissemination are discussed.

Stage X: Tracking Outcomes

Although not a formal part of research, we include here the step of assessing outcomes. This step is particularly germane to I/O work, where outcomes frequently occur in two domains.

Except in explicitly action-oriented research, insider research partners tend to have agendas somewhat different from those of outside researchers. Insiders are more often concerned about improved practice in their local situations, whereas outsiders are more often concerned about contributing to knowledge beyond the immediate situation. When both scholarly and practical agendas are pertinent, how well the research addresses both parties' aims is a measure of the effectiveness of their joint study. It also may be a good indicator of the likelihood that they will wish to work together again.

Some I/O projects succeed in addressing the multiple and differing concerns of insiders and outsiders. For example, the disabilities advocacy study succeeded in advancing scholarly goals and in improving the practice of the advisory board involved in the study. The inside researchers attributed this to the fact that although the outside researcher alone collected the data, she did so according to data collection plans that were created jointly. Moreover, insiders remained in the setting to implement proposed changes based on the study's results. The fact that setting insiders are often "permanent" members of the setting means that they typically are in a position to have much more influence over activities taking place in the setting than are outsiders (including consultants). In the prenatal evaluation study, program participants who became Whitmore's co-researchers reported feeling "enlivened" and "empowered" by their work on the study. Similar outcomes occurred in the Merrifield (1993) and Comstock and Fox (1993) studies.

In a thoughtful discussion of the dilemmas involved in dealing with different sets of interests and agendas, Israel and her colleagues (1992) trace how differences between research and action components of a joint labor-management project may create tensions between researchers and employees. On several occasions, when the outside researchers suggested collecting additional data, the inside research partners were hesitant because they believed that employees had not yet seen enough results from the previous data collection effort. Moreover, there were points at which outside researchers placed much more emphasis on data collection for basic research and evaluation purposes than the inside researchers considered appropriate.

As this discussion indicates, even when there is joint insider and outsider involvement and influence during many stages of a research project, there is no guarantee that the aims of both insiders and outsiders will be met. Insiders and outsiders need to be aware of the multiple constituencies represented among as well as beyond them. Even with the difficulties encountered, however, the likelihood that both parties' stated interests are taken into consideration is greater for I/O research than for research conducted solely by an outside researcher.

4. AN EXTENDED EXAMPLE OF INSIDER/OUTSIDER TEAM RESEARCH

I think the inside/outside researchers here can help us a lot (comment during a group reflection period by one of the participants in the Faculty Development Committee study).

In Chapter 3, we broke down the research process, suggesting what I/O team research would look like at each of several stages. In this chapter, we "reassemble" the process by presenting a firsthand account of one of Jean Bartunek's experiences of insider/outsider collaboration. Through this in-depth look "behind the scenes," we are able to fill in details about I/O work not usually included in published research accounts. Jean describes the research in her own voice.

The Faculty Development Committee

The I/O work I will discuss is part of a long-term field research project on a group called the Faculty Development Committee (FDC). The FDC is a seven-member group of teachers within a Network of schools. It was established to "empower" teachers in the Network. By this, the group's founders meant, generally, providing opportunities for teachers to develop skill in articulating and communicating their practical knowledge to one another and in the public realm. Data collection regarding the FDC began in 1988 and was completed in 1995. Funding for the data collection has been provided by the Network of schools as well as by grants from Boston College, and writing about the group is still in progress. I will begin by explaining how the joint I/O work came about and the philosophy of the FDC. The philosophy is important, because much of the research done on the group has aimed at exploring how its philosophy affected members' work and decision making. Then I will describe the general process of conducting research on the group and specific processes associated with two of the studies in this research program. The chapter concludes with some observations about the FDC project as well as a link back to the stages discussed in Chapter 3.

DEVELOPING THE INSIDER/
OUTSIDER RESEARCH TEAM

In 1988, Catherine Lacey, a friend of mine who formerly had taught and served as an administrator in a national Network of independent schools, was a doctoral student. She and a friend of hers, Diane Wood, who at the time was an administrator in one of the Network schools, were planning to establish a committee, the FDC, that would be composed primarily of experienced teachers and aimed at empowering teachers in the Network. Diane and Catherine had participated in a Network task force to review a number of initiatives that had taken place in the Network in recent years. The task force had concluded that experienced teachers in the Network were being "left behind" somewhat in these initiatives. Diane and Catherine were determined to change this pattern. They were committed to establishing the FDC in a way that would respond to the desires of experienced teachers rather than imposing administrators' plans on them. They believed that the FDC had the potential to make important contributions both to the Network and to educational reform efforts in the United States. As a result, they thought that it could be useful to collect data on its activities.

Catherine and Diane recognized that they were not experienced researchers. They also were concerned that taking on a research agenda might interfere with their practical agenda of establishing and leading the group. Catherine thought that I might be able to help them learn something about publishing and also be able to work with them to collect data about the group in a way that would be beneficial to it. Catherine and I talked about several ways that I might be involved in the research, and I eventually suggested that she, Diane, and I study the early development of the committee together using a joint insider/outsider approach. That is, we would collect different but complementary sets of data about the group and do joint writing about it. I gave Catherine and Diane the Evered and Louis (1981) article as a model of differences in perspective insiders and outsiders might bring to this project.

Catherine and Diane expressed concern that they might end up devoting too much of their attention to formal research tasks rather than guiding the group. I suggested that I could do the "formal" data collection and that their own data collection should focus on their own experiences in the group. That is, the two of them should reflect on their experiences, both discussing them with each other and keeping written journal records of their own interpretations of events. We agreed that I, as an outside researcher, would sit in and take notes at the three or four FDC meetings that would occur each year. I would also tape-record a reflection session at the end of each meeting, during which FDC members would discuss what had gone well and poorly at each meeting as well as the implications for their work together. I would then send a transcript of the reflection session back to the FDC members for their own notes. I would also contact the FDC leaders before FDC meetings to learn ahead of time what they intended to do at the meetings, then contact them afterward to see how they felt the meetings had gone. Finally, I would conduct phone interviews with the other members of the FDC twice a year. Diane and Catherine made a commitment to record their individual and joint reflections on the meetings and to keep journals of FDC-related events.

INITIAL CONTRACTING WITH THE FDC MEMBERS

In preparation for the first formal meeting of the FDC, in October 1988, I prepared a formal written document outlining the research plan and rationale. Catherine and Diane introduced the idea to the other FDC members during the group's first meeting. The other FDC members were interested in the proposal, seeing it as a way to ensure reflection in the group. They agreed to allow research to be conducted on the FDC. I joined them for the end of their first meeting, and Catherine conducted the first taped reflection session at its conclusion.

From then until the end of the 1994-1995 school year, I sat in as an outside nonparticipant observer at FDC meetings and other FDC activities, such as institutes the FDC members conducted for experienced faculty in the Network. During this time, the FDC experienced several planned changes in membership. Diane resigned from the group in 1990, after the group's second year. Catherine resigned the leadership of the group that same year but remained a member of the group until 1994. All the original group members and many of those who succeeded them have now been replaced.

PHILOSOPHY AND ACTIVITIES OF THE FDC

Catherine and Diane's philosophy for the FDC focused on empowering teachers to make a public contribution in the Network and in the broader educational reform debate (Lacey, Wood, & Bartunek, 1990). This original philosophy has been retained. Underlying this philosophy was a belief, consistent with the teacher-researcher movement, that if given the opportunity to build relationships with colleagues, tell and hear stories of one another's professional experiences, and articulate their own challenges and problems, teachers can grow in awareness of the knowledge gleaned from their work and of their power to imagine together new ways of educating. Catherine and Diane also believed that from this affirmation of teachers' value would emerge a desire to communicate their knowledge to wider audiences. They further believed that improvement in education hinges on providing forums for teachers to articulate and communicate their practical, classroom-based knowledge to one another and in the public realm. Relatedly, they saw teachers as having few opportunities to participate in the communities of inquiry characteristic of other professions (cf. Grumet, 1988), through which more public contributions are generated.

Catherine and Diane envisioned the FDC as a forum through which committee members and an ever-widening circle of teachers could live out this philosophy. To implement their vision, they introduced relatively novel group processes into the FDC's functioning. For example, FDC meetings begin with members sharing narratives of their professional experiences, such as of "a powerful mentor" or of "a teaching experience that changed me." This narrative sharing both establishes a reflective tone and links the work members do during the meeting to the daily experiences of teachers. The teachers participating in the FDC have described this sharing of narratives both as personally empowering and as ensuring that their work during the meeting stays connected with teachers' actual experience. Catherine wrote a doctoral dissertation on teachers' narratives during the early years of the group (Lacey, 1991).

The FDC reaches other Network faculty members through two primary activities. It sponsors an annual journal of teacher writing to which all Network faculty members may submit articles. In addition, it has conducted a series of faculty institutes aimed at bringing teachers from the Network schools together to develop proposals for faculty development.

SUMMARY OF PRODUCTS OF THE JOINT WORK

Catherine, Diane, and I have examined and written about the FDC in several forums to this point. In all of our studies and writings, we have explored the relationship between the stated purposes and philosophy of the FDC and particular activities and practices in which the group has been involved. We wrote a paper about the FDC's philosophy, rationale, and practices during its first year that was presented to the American Educational Research Association (Lacey et al., 1990). We wrote about dynamics of the first faculty institute sponsored by the FDC, an occasion on which a number of misperceptions surfaced among FDC members about the leaders' intentions (Bartunek et al., 1992). The two FDC members who replaced Catherine and Diane as leaders joined us in examining and writing about the FDC's first leadership succession process (Bartunek, Galosy, Lacey, Lies, & Wood, 1991). In another instance, Catherine and I documented the group's experiences in dealing with an alcoholic member (Bartunek & Lacey, 1993). Catherine examined the FDC's approach to empowerment (Lacey, 1995). In addition, Diane and Catherine worked together to document the philosophy of the group (Wood & Lacey, 1991). Data collection processes that served as the basis for each of the collaborative works primarily consisted of the strategies outlined above: I collected relatively formal observational data and interview data while the insider members of the research team maintained journals documenting their experiences with the FDC and reflections on them.

The FDC research illustrates how, in the course of ongoing field research, issues emerge—such as leadership succession or dealing with an alcoholic member—as the life of the group unfolds. These issues provide the impetus for and focus of deeper study and subsequent distinct research reports. They do so by virtue of attracting the attention of both group members and the outside researcher.

This chapter will focus on how Catherine, Diane, their successors, and I worked together to study the first leadership succession that occurred in the FDC. It will also look at my work with Catherine in studying and writing about how the group dealt with an alcoholic member. We hope that by exploring these two specific projects within a larger research project in the same field setting, the reader will come away with a picture of the interactions, mechanics, and issues that emerge in actually doing I/O team research.

THE FDC'S FIRST LEADERSHIP SUCCESSION

Events Associated With the First Leadership Succession

The original plan of the FDC was that after two years, Catherine and Diane would resign their leadership roles but remain as members of the FDC. FDC members agreed that a decision about the first leadership succession would be made during the January meeting of the group's second year, 1990.

During the January 1990 meeting, Diane decided that because of other commitments she needed to resign as a member of the FDC as well as resigning as a leader. She told Catherine this one night in a private conversation, then told the rest of the group the next morning. The particular FDC session in which this was discussed was difficult and awkward for everyone present. In addition to dealing with Diane's decision to resign, the group dealt with decisions about its form of leadership (whether it should continue with the coleadership model Catherine and Diane had established) and who the new leader(s) should be. Initially, FDC members were uncertain what to do, and no one volunteered to assume leadership. Diane became upset with the group. She felt that if the group truly had been empowering, the members would take more initiative in volunteering to lead. After a lengthy and awkward discussion, the group decided to continue coleadership roles. On the basis of self-nomination, Jodie Galosy and Betty Lies were chosen to take these roles. In their taped reflections at the end of the meeting, the FDC members all said clearly that they strongly valued the approach the founders of the group had taken. One commented, for example, that in founding the FDC Catherine and Diane had "saved the Network."

In the spring of 1990, Diane and Catherine had a meeting with Jodie and Betty to discuss how they might assume the leadership of the group. At this meeting, Jodie and Betty made it evident that they valued Catherine and Diane's work and were excited about continuing their philosophy; that was a main reason they had decided to continue coleadership roles. In fact, on the occasion of this meeting, Betty, who is an English teacher and poet, wrote a poem praising the ways the founders had acted.

Writing the Paper

The leadership succession seemed sufficiently interesting and unique among succession processes that I proposed writing about it in conjunction with both Catherine and Diane, as outgoing leaders, and Jodie and Betty, as incoming leaders. I made this suggestion during the summer following the transition events but before the FDC had begun meeting under Jodie and Betty's leadership. All four agreed.

The major question we addressed in the study was whether leadership succession in the FDC had mirrored normal processes in groups not designed to be empowering. A frequent pattern in more traditional groups is successor denigration of the outgoing leaders and their ideas (Gephart, 1978; Heller, 1989). Had this same pattern occurred in the FDC?

Our joint reflection on the processes that had occurred in the group suggested that, in the long run, the succession process in the FDC was much more affirming of the founders than is usually the case when there is a change in leadership in a group. This had been illustrated, for example, in Betty and Jodie's decision to follow the original leadership model. It appeared that the FDC's focus on empowerment made a difference in its internal processes, in that the next leaders did not reject the original pattern. During the January 1990 FDC meeting to discuss succession, however, the founders did not experience the process as affirming; rather, they questioned how successful they had been at empowering the group. The five of us prepared a paper suggesting a number of reasons for and implications of this discrepancy, noting in particular differences in ways the founders and other FDC members were understanding concepts of empowerment. I wrote the first draft, and the four others made revisions. I then rewrote the paper, incorporating the suggested revisions, and submitted it to the Eastern Academy of Management, where it was presented and published in the proceedings. Thus, the insiders and I contributed jointly to the scholarly development of the paper.

The Insiders' Contributions to the Paper

My first draft of the paper omitted important information about events that occurred and FDC members' responses to them—information I was unfamiliar with. I wrote what I could as a beginning, and insider members filled in missing information and made corrections. Types of contributions insiders made to the paper included the following:

The insiders made factual corrections. For example, I had recorded the founders' original plans about remaining on the committee incorrectly; the insiders corrected this.

The insiders expressed issues and feelings of the group that were not voiced during the course of decision making about the leadership succession. For example, one of the insiders indicated that she had not said anything during the discussion because she was "struggling with wanting to be a coleader, but wondering whether (she) could possibly measure up." All I had seen was that this insider member was silent.

They gave rationales for negative events described in the first draft. For example, Diane explained why she had become upset at the group.

They added their unique style to the report. For example, Betty included the poem she had written about the founders. Poetry is not ordinarily included in scholarly social science reports.

These and other contributions made by the insiders were incorporated into the final draft of the report, strengthening it considerably. In particular, their changes introduced cognitions and feelings not formally articulated in the group or easily observable, but having a strong impact on member experiences.

Practical Impacts of the Paper

Beyond illustrating dynamics of leadership succession that have not been discussed in prior research on the topic, the report had an impact within the FDC. The impact was noted first by Jodie and Betty, the new leaders, who began their work while the paper was being written. Shortly after receiving the first draft, Betty sent a note to Jodie and me in which she commented that the draft had caused her to think about leadership in the FDC in a new way. She commented on

how carefully the group is looking at us as their leaders. Realizing this started me thinking about what I think is a paradox, or even a contradiction, in the way we're defining collaborative leadership. . . . The way leadership is set up now, collaborative leadership means, in reality, the two leaders collaborating, not really a sharing of leadership among all the members of the group. . . . I wonder if we haven't created a mystique of leadership on the committee, which we might examine, to see if there are ways of lessening it.

The FDC was due to experience its second leadership succession shortly before the paper would be presented at the convention. I sent copies of the paper to the FDC members, and Betty distributed her commentary. After reading the paper and Betty's commentary, newer FDC members suggested during the second succession discussion that the leadership form be changed to be more fully participative among all the group members. FDC members agreed that rather than having two designated coleaders of the group, there be one coordinator, who would have responsibility primarily for coordinating with the Network office. All the members would take turns convening the group and carrying out other roles the leaders previously had filled, such as keeping minutes. Moreover, the agenda for each upcoming meeting, along with who would carry out each role during it, would be established through group discussion at the prior meeting. The FDC immediately began working in that manner. Thus, one outcome of the study was a substantial change in the division of labor among group members. The more collaborative leadership structure created among FDC members at that meeting remains in place several years later.

The insider members of the research team examining leadership succession told me that the process of analysis and writing made them more aware of their underlying assumptions and concerns, as well as providing a clearer picture of the succession. Out of the joint reflective process came a substantial and useful awareness that was described in a scholarly presentation of dynamics underlying succession and that also provoked a rethinking of how leadership would be handled in the group, bringing practice into closer alignment with the group's philosophy and mission.

UNDERSTANDING THE DYNAMICS ASSOCIATED WITH CONFRONTING AN ALCOHOLIC MEMBER

Events Associated With the Confrontation

Later in the FDC's existence, three new members joined the group. The other FDC members soon became aware that one of them, Evelyn (a pseudonym), had a serious drinking problem. At the second meeting of the group that year, several FDC members decided to confront Evelyn with her abuse of alcohol and make provisions for her to go for treatment. Most, but not all, group members were involved in the planning and conduct of the intervention, which they coordinated with Evelyn's family and school. The formal intervention itself went smoothly and was successful, in that Evelyn entered treatment and then returned to her job and work. The events surrounding it, however, were emotion filled and difficult for FDC members. Evelyn remained in the FDC for the remainder of the academic year, until she resigned from her job at her school.

As most of the FDC members began planning the intervention, I was faced with a dilemma. As an outside researcher, I saw this as an important moment in the group's life, one obviously amenable to research. I also believed that what was happening with Evelyn was personally crucial and did not want the research to interfere with events surrounding the intervention. I did not, in other words, think it appropriate to take notes, if these would interfere with the intervention process. Consequently, I decided to play a behind-the-scenes role. For example, prior to the intervention, I obtained a list of treatment centers in the city where Evelyn lived and gave these to the FDC members. During the intervention, I told Evelyn that her life was more important to me than a study, and that one of the ways I could contribute to it was not to take any notes on the events there. At the time of the intervention, none of us associated with it planned to write about it.

Eight months after the intervention occurred, shortly before she decided to resign from her teaching position, Evelyn asked Catherine and me to write about the intervention. She had been very impressed with Catherine's (Lacey, 1991) dissertation work on narrative as well as the narrative sharing in which the FDC members engaged at the beginning of every meeting. She felt that telling the story of what had happened to her during the intervention would be true to the spirit of the FDC.

In this case, the data collection, so to speak, was done retrospectively. After talking with Evelyn, I wrote down everything I could remember about the events surrounding the intervention and circulated my notes to Evelyn and other relevant group members. I asked them to fill in missing information. Although Evelyn did not respond, most of the other group members did. They supplied numerous recollections about the events and included personal feelings that had arisen as the intervention was planned and conducted, as well as afterward. Together, Catherine and I wrote several drafts of a paper telling the story of the intervention and its aftermath. The paper focused in part on how the sharing of stories enabled Evelyn to trust the group and helped the other group members to think that Evelyn could trust them to be acting out of concern for her. It also addressed how the story of the intervention became embedded for a time in the story group members told about the group to newcomers. We also included analysis of a number of the contradictions in the group's dynamics surrounding the intervention and its aftermath (for example, that although inclusion was a strong aim of the FDC, some members were included and others excluded in the planning for the intervention).

After several drafts had been completed, Catherine and I sent a copy of the paper to all FDC members, asking for their comments. Most of the members did not respond to this draft, having given us their input on the earlier draft. Evelyn did respond this time, sending 10 single-spaced typewritten pages of notes in which she sketched out more fully her role and feelings in the process. For example, whereas other FDC members had discussed how the intervention gave them a sense of working together very effectively, Evelyn noted that she had been very effectively excluded as the "target" of their work. Catherine and I incorporated Evelyn's experience as we revised the paper.

The Process of Writing the Paper

The process of writing this paper differed from the process of writing about the leadership succession for several reasons: We had more time for writing, the study was more complex, and there were only two authors. For this paper, Catherine and I alternated writing drafts. We found that we tended to emphasize different dimensions. Catherine tended to emphasize internal dimensions, especially the role stories had played in the group's decision to intervene, whereas I tended to look at what had happened from the outside in, focusing on dynamics present but not acknowledged in the group's process.

Contrary to the leadership succession paper, for which other authors added essentially complementary information, the process of joint work on this paper was conflictual and difficult. We argued strongly about the relative importance of our different perspectives. In talking through our differences, new insights were generated. One of our learnings, for example, was that my external emphasis could be integrated with the approach to stories Catherine was taking, as I indicate below.

When Evelyn had asked that the intervention be written about, the group's assumption was that it had been a success, in large part because Evelyn went into treatment. As we worked on the paper and received feedback from other group members, however, several complications of the intervention and its aftermath emerged. For example, one member noted that she had been left out of the planning process and was tempted to quit the group. In addition, some members felt badly about how they had interacted with Evelyn when she returned to the FDC following the intervention; they therefore questioned its success. Perhaps because the effort to get Evelyn into treatment had succeeded, group members were hesitant to talk at the time about subsequent dilemmas they had experienced. As they commented on drafts of the paper, the story Catherine was interested in pursuing developed considerably, and the kinds of underlying dynamics present in the group that I was particularly interested in began to surface. Thus, it was possible to include in the paper descriptions both of how the story of the intervention had evolved in being written and rewritten, and of how the group had experienced multiple, intertwined, contradictory dilemmas. It is unlikely that this information would have been known as fully if group members had not participated in constructing the story of the intervention and its aftermath. At the time of this writing, the final scholarly account of this event is still being constructed.

Some Observations

As revealed by changes the insiders suggested to the leadership succession paper, it is easy for an outside researcher to misinterpret insiders' behaviors, either by missing nuances while relating apparent facts or by only partially appreciating actors' perspectives. Thus, outside researchers are helped in portraying the situation as insiders flesh out their experiences of events.

As is suggested in the alcoholism intervention paper, outsiders and insiders also may interpret situations differently. This may occur if insiders are personally involved or simply because insiders and outsiders operate from different vantage points. Outsiders are more likely to emphasize general analytic dimensions, whereas insiders focus on the processes in which they have been engaged. Moreover, different members of a group may have different experiences of what ostensibly is the same event. Such differences must be dealt with openly. The "ideal" outcome of openly addressing differences is the development of a new perspective that goes beyond both insiders' and outsiders' original viewpoints, such as the new ways of understanding Catherine and I sometimes achieved in working through our disagreements in the alcoholism intervention paper. If and when an impasse is reached, it is valuable to report both perspectives and the disagreement between them rather than present a false compromise.

Analysis of the FDC Research
in Terms of I/O Research Stages

STAGE I: COMPOSING THE I/O RESEARCH TEAM

In the case of the FDC work, this stage had a number of dimensions. The idea of working jointly on the research was first articulated by Catherine, after which Jean suggested the form it would take. When the FDC began, it was necessary that a contracting process be repeated with all the group members.

The two specific papers described here were initiated for different reasons. Jean explicitly initiated the leadership succession study, whereas the alcohol intervention study was initiated at the request of the group member who was the focal point of the intervention. In both papers, all the FDC members involved directly in the study events were included in some ways, through coauthorship (Bartunek et al., 1991) or through commenting on drafts (Bartunek & Lacey, 1993).

STAGE II: DEVELOPING A WORKING RELATIONSHIP

It was necessary to build a working relationship among the coauthors. Jean, Catherine, and Diane initially spent considerable time together working out the details of what the joint I/O work would mean for the FDC, particularly with respect to how Diane and Catherine would lead the group as opposed to conducting formal data gathering activities. The specific working relationship for the leadership succession paper was relatively simple: Given time constraints associated with a convention, Jean sent the draft of the paper to her coauthors and then incorporated their comments in a revision. The working relationship in the alcoholism intervention paper was more complex, necessitating that Catherine and Jean develop an initial agreement about writing the paper and then work out subsequent disagreements until they could incorporate both of their perspectives.

STAGE III: FORMULATING RESEARCH
QUESTIONS TO ORIENT THE STUDY

The general research question addressed in all the studies of the FDC, how the philosophy of the group has an impact on its practice, was developed jointly by Jean, Catherine, and Diane. In the leadership succession study, Jean formulated the specific research questions addressed in terms of leadership succession literature. In the alcoholism intervention study, Jean and

Catherine together formulated the specific research questions addressed. We saw, however, that they tended to focus on somewhat different questions. Catherine focused more on group processes, and Jean attended more to external, analytical issues.

STAGE IV: DESIGNING DATA COLLECTION PROCESSES

Jean, Catherine, and Diane together designed the general data collection processes in the succession study. Jean made formal observations and conducted interviews, and the insider collaborators contributed their journal notes. With some modifications, this general pattern was maintained throughout the course of study of the FDC.

STAGE V: COLLECTING DATA

In both studies we have discussed, the outsider and insiders contributed crucial data. In the succession study, Jean took notes at formal meetings of the full FDC but was unaware of all the experiences of the people present there. Moreover, she was not present at the meeting the two founders had with their successors. The four leaders provided the only record of that meeting. Betty's poem proved to be yet another source of data, conveying her experience of the situation. In the alcoholism study, Jean's recollections provided the foundation, the first draft of what had occurred, but it was crucial that various members of the FDC supplied accounts of their own experiences and interpretations of the events that occurred.

STAGES VI AND VII: ANALYZING AND INTERPRETING DATA AND WRITING REPORTS AND PRESENTING RESULTS

These two stages were largely intertwined in both papers, in that analysis of events was carried out primarily within the process of writing about them. Jean wrote the draft of the leadership succession paper, which included a first draft of her analysis of events. The insider members of the research team then suggested modifications in the analysis and the report. Jean and Catherine, in succeeding drafts of the alcoholism paper, worked to analyze the events that occurred. In doing so, we saw that they sometimes tended to emphasize somewhat different analytic dimensions. The conflict of interpretations opened up new ways of seeing events that had occurred.

The writing of both papers involved multiple drafts, shared with all those involved in the events. In the leadership succession paper, all major players participated in developing the story that was told. In the alcohol intervention situation, all relevant members of the FDC were sent two different drafts of the paper and were encouraged to comment and reflect on the drafts. Throughout the FDC studies, attempts have been made to offer those involved extensive opportunities to add their own interpretations of events under study.

STAGE VIII: TAKING ACTION

The FDC research project has had primarily scholarly aims, so taking action has not been a primary goal. However, action was taken as a result of the leadership succession paper. Working on the paper got the new leaders and then the members to rethink the role of leadership in the FDC, and thus to revise this role when the next leadership succession opportunity occurred. This provoked a major change in the group's life. Joint action was not taken as a result of the alcohol intervention paper, in part because by the time of writing of the paper, Evelyn had rotated off membership in the FDC. Writing the paper did cause several of the group members to rethink the way they had acted toward Evelyn, in particular to question whether the intervention approach they had taken had been consistent with the group's philosophy.

STAGE IX: MAKING SCHOLARLY CONTRIBUTIONS

Both papers made some type of scholarly contribution. The primary contribution of the leadership succession study was a demonstrated contrast between the type of leadership succession processes that occurred in this group and processes in other groups that have different types of orienting philosophies. The study also generated reflections on how the philosophy of the FDC affected this process. The primary scholarly contribution of the alcohol intervention study was an analysis of ways that stories about an event can evolve over time and how their evolution can bring to the surface contradictory dynamics present in a group but typically hidden from the members' view.

STAGE X: TRACKING OUTCOMES

The two instances of I/O team research with the FDC discussed here have begun to have some scholarly impact, as papers about them have been presented to professional audiences. Writing about them continues. As previously noted, the report on the leadership succession had a clear impact on the FDC's organizational practices. The study of the alcohol intervention also had an impact, as members reflected on events and looked more deeply at the complicated dynamics associated with the intervention than they otherwise might have done. One effect of I/O team research in this group was a deeper insight on the part of insider members about their own experiences.

Conclusion

In this chapter, we considered an extended example of two efforts within one larger study using insider/outsider team research. Our examples suggest that insiders' sources of knowledge often may add considerably to outsiders' understandings and that insiders' reflection and practice may benefit from their participation in research endeavors that have primarily a scholarly orientation. The material here indicates one way this joint work may be conducted; as we have made evident, it suggests rather than exhausts the wide range of possibilities for I/O work. We hope that this close look at these studies sparks readers' imaginations to consider ways insiders and outsiders may be involved in I/O joint work and some of the issues attendant to doing so.

5. PRACTICAL AND ETHICAL CHALLENGES OF I/O TEAM RESEARCH

In an article describing potential tensions between researchers and community-based practitioners, Nyden and Wiewel (1992, pp. 46-47) wrote,

> Researchers and community activists or practitioners . . . do not necessarily view the research process in the same way. CBOs (community-based organizations) are often caught up in the day-to-day realities of running an organization and providing services to a community. There is pressure to use what precious resources are available in "doing" something that needs to be done, not in "doing research" about what needs to be done. There are also often power imbalances in the research-CBO relationship. . . . This relationship . . . can be the foundation for collaborative research, but it can also be the basis for a researcher taking advantage of a CBO's needs, doing the research, and using it for discipline-oriented ends rather than community improvement.

This quotation, while not addressed directly to I/O research teams, illustrates well the kinds of tensions that can arise within such teams. I/O teams can be very productive, but along the way difficulties often arise because of the divergence in perspectives the team is seeking to encompass.

If we have been clear thus far, readers should have a handle on what I/O work looks like and the practicalities of using I/O approaches to inquiry. At this point, it is time to qualify the case. Here we consider obstacles and challenges—both practical and ethical—in doing I/O work as well as when it may be inappropriate or impractical to do so.

Practical Challenges in Doing I/O Team Research

There are a number of potential problems associated with doing I/O work. Some are those that any team might encounter (Dyer, 1987; Hackman, 1990) simply because several different people are working together. Other problems, however, are associated with the fact that it is insiders and outsiders who are working together. Here we consider four common challenges germane to I/O work associated, respectively, with gaining access to the research site, managing the interpersonal differences that arise from the heterogeneity of theorizing, maintaining the separation between team members necessary to produce a marginal perspective, and disseminating findings to multiple audiences.

ACCESS TO THE RESEARCH SITE: APPEARANCES, ALLIANCES, AND INDEPENDENCE

In many types of I/O team research, access to settings is facilitated simply because particular setting members are part of the research team. Such membership may not be sufficient if some relevant and powerful subgroups are not represented on the research team (Israel et al., 1992; Lampton & Tunstill, 1994). Moreover, when there is strong division in the setting, if the insiders represent only a portion of the factions, there will be problems achieving adequate access. When there are multiple factions, outside researchers in most of the research approaches we discuss should attempt to include insiders from multiple groups as co-researchers or, when this cannot be accomplished, create links with these other groups themselves. In contrast, we have seen that, in participatory research, the research team deliberately includes the historically disenfranchised while excluding members of the dominant group. In I/O research, facilitating wider access to information held by more powerful groups may be one of the aims of the research process.

HETEROGENEITY AND THE
CHALLENGE OF MANAGING DIFFERENCES

The very differences in perspective between insiders and outsiders around which their joint work is structured often are associated with differences in values, experience, and even communication styles (Ellis, 1994; Israel et al., 1992). These, in turn, may lead to conflicts among team members about the meaning and causes of organizational events. For example, as we indicated in Chapter 4, Jean Bartunek and Catherine Lacey had quite different views of what they should emphasize in their study of how the Faculty Development Committee dealt with an alcoholic member.

For joint I/O work to be successful, team members must be willing to make intellectual shifts. Outside researchers must work to appreciate insiders' mind-sets, and insiders must work to appreciate outsiders' points of view. Both must be willing and able to deal directly with conflicts that arise among them, whether the conflicts are cognitive, value based, or interest based. If team members avoid conflict or rely solely on compromise, substantive results of the study may be weakened and team members may become dispirited.

PRODUCING MARGINALITY BY MAINTAINING
SEPARATION BETWEEN TEAM MEMBERS

Another challenge in doing I/O work is to ensure that together the insiders and outsiders create a marginal perspective, one in which neither party tries to approach the research exactly as the other party does. The temptation is for outside researchers to become caught up in insiders' understandings and for inside researchers to try to adopt the outsider's analytical approach. If the outsider "goes native" or the insider "goes stranger," however, gains previously possible are compromised. I/O work is not about converting the parties' perspectives or even about supplementing one party's perspective with that of the other; rather, I/O work is about each party achieving an appreciation and healthy respect for the other's positioned perspective even while valuing his own. This is a tall order, but accomplishing it is aided by recognizing both that it is difficult and why it is necessary.

Problems arise when either party takes on the other's perspective. In identifying with insiders, outsiders may be tempted to gloss over controversial issues in the setting that are pertinent to the study. In identifying with outsiders, insiders may be tempted to accept uncritically outsiders' categorizations for behavior, rather than contributing their own unique perspective. Problems also arise if researchers curtail their efforts to appreciate the other's approach. Either response will reduce the extent to which team members continue contributing observations and interpretations grounded in different perspectives. Successful joint I/O research requires insiders and outsiders to maintain both their own perspective and their appreciation for, respect for, and distance from another perspective.

DISSEMINATING FINDINGS: MULTIPLE AUDIENCES, MULTIPLE MESSAGES

There also are potential problems regarding internal and external dissemination of findings. With regard to external, especially academic, dissemination, insider members may be relatively unfamiliar with the scholarly norms necessary for an academic presentation and so initially may feel left out of writing (e.g., Whitmore, 1994). It is then necessary for outsiders to structure ways that insiders can best make their own contribution to presentations of results. For example, as Whitmore did, an outside researcher might write a first draft of a paper and then encourage insider critiques of and additions to it.

There also may be problems in disseminating results within the setting. Setting members may have expectations that an insider or an outsider who has collaborated extensively with insiders will present positive findings, at least to a greater extent than would a researcher who is solely an outsider. Whyte (1993, 1994) faced this situation when setting members were upset at some of the things he wrote in *Street Corner Society,* even though they thought that events were depicted accurately and even though Whyte had not disclosed the identity of the setting or its members. Setting members who become close to a researcher often expect that the researcher will not air their "dirty linen." Dealing with this expectation while at the same time presenting findings as truthfully as possible may be quite difficult.

None of the practical challenges discussed here necessarily represents a fatal flaw in a specific research project. In order to gain the advantages of I/O collaborations, however, a research team needs to address the challenges attendant to this approach.

Ethical Challenges in Conducting I/O Team Research

Three ethical dilemmas are likely to arise when conducting I/O work. The first dilemma concerns the *informed consent* of those participating in the research. As a general principle, informed consent ensures that participants in a study understand what the study entails and are able to make a decision to participate based on that understanding. Informed consent with regard to many joint I/O studies, however, is problematic. Prospective participants often do not have full knowledge—nor do inside *or* outside researchers—of the types of events that will unfold during a study, particularly a qualitative study (Howe & Dougherty, 1993). Informed consent in many joint I/O studies must then reflect an awareness that such events cannot entirely be predicted. As a result, a revised view of informed consent seems warranted, in which consent is negotiated at different points in the research cycle. Informed consent is not something that can be handled once and for all at the beginning of a study.

A second ethical dilemma concerns *deception.* In some research modes, deception is relatively easy to detect. For example, a researcher in a laboratory study might misrepresent conditions of the study to a research participant. Although in joint I/O research such blatant deception is unlikely to occur, more subtle forms of deception may arise. For example, as the relationship between researchers and research participants becomes closer, either outside or inside researchers may hesitate to remind participants that the research being conducted remains the primary reason for their interacting. Thus, even if participants are told at the outset that one aim of the research is to produce a series of papers or a book, participants may ignore or forget about such a goal and consequently feel deceived or betrayed when a publication appears (e.g., Whyte, 1994). These feelings are likely to be intense if the report is not flattering. Reactions to such tacit deception may be particularly strong from setting members who are not part of the research team. They are likely to be directed toward the insider researchers, whom they tacitly expect to be more positive about the setting. It is important for researchers, both insider and outsider, to keep the aims of the study public and salient. This will foster the ongoing negotiation of informed consent and will decrease the likelihood that research participants feel deceived by later publication of findings.

Confidentiality represents a third ethical dilemma, one that is particularly relevant in presenting results of joint I/O studies. Confidentiality may be sufficiently difficult to maintain that it may impede joint I/O publication of reports (Ledford & Mohrman, 1993). Information about possible complex outcomes of a study, at least as much as can be envisaged, should be addressed openly early in the research effort, with researchers and participants together discussing the importance of accuracy. Participants should be afforded a chance to respond to drafts of study reports, as was provided in the Bartunek and Lacey study. Members of the research team may need to facilitate discussions about the issues among setting members. The drafts, in essence, can be treated as a kind of feedback mechanism.

If setting members wish to maintain public anonymity, researchers and other participants can agree to alter some less important details of the report in order to mask the identity of the setting but not misrepresent essential features of the setting studied. They might, for example, alter the location of the setting or the gender or other personal characteristics of characters, if these features are not germane to the subject matter of the study. If necessary, they may alter the affiliation of inside researchers, such as associating them with a university rather than their workplace.

Sometimes, however, public anonymity may not be appropriate. As in the case of the disabilities advocacy study, insider researchers may feel no need to keep the name of their setting confidential. In PAR or participatory research studies, such as those at Xerox, North Bonneville, and Kingsport, part of the researchers' aims may be to publicize the site. No single approach to confidentiality is appropriate for all occasions. Researchers need to be clear about implications of whichever approach they take. Sometimes a setting is not given credit for impressive events if anonymity is maintained. Sometimes, however, for liability and other reasons, it is crucial to keep the setting disguised.

When to Use Insider/Outsider Research Teams

There are some contexts in which I/O research teams are particularly appropriate and others in which they are not. Sometimes an I/O approach is not possible even when a researcher desires it. One obvious condition for effective I/O team research is a match between the aims of outside researchers and the interests of inside researchers. That is, all must see the possibility of meeting at least some of their needs through the prospective joint inquiry. A second condition is a qualified and willing set of potential insider and outsider team members. What constitutes "qualified" will depend on the type of research anticipated and the focus of the study. Thus, for example, Whitmore needed as insider research participants mothers who had been participating in the prenatal programs and who were reliable and not afraid to talk with strangers. For the developmental disabilities study, Bartunek needed co-researchers who would be involved in all stages of the research, including formulation of the conceptual foundation of the study, study design, data analysis, conceptual formulation, and the writing up of the research results.

There are some occasions when joint I/O work is of particular value for outsiders. For example, Lampton and Tunstill (1994) note that for outsiders doing research with aboriginal groups, group acceptance of the outside researcher is crucial. This can come about much more easily when the outsider is conducting the research jointly with insiders. Joint I/O work was necessary for Bartunek to understand the rationale, assumptions, and feelings operating in the FDC at the time of both the first leadership succession and the alcoholism intervention.

There also are some occasions when joint I/O research is of particular value for insiders. In the case of action research, participatory research, or PAR, outside assistance is sought as a means of helping to solve a particular problem. In the case of more basic scholarly work, insiders may wish to publish but be unfamiliar with how to do so. This was part of the reason Jean Bartunek, Catherine Lacey, and Diane Wood initiated the joint work described in Chapter 4. Sometimes insiders prefer to have someone who is seen as "independent" or "neutral" involved with them in studying a setting (e.g., Israel et al., 1992). As is the case with many aboriginal peoples, because of past experiences of exploitation by outside researchers (Diamond & Polansky, 1994), insiders may want to make sure that their own voice is heard.

There also are occasions when joint insider/outsider research, or at least joint I/O publication, is inappropriate or unworkable. It does not make sense to undertake joint I/O work when, for example, there are seemingly irreconcilable value differences between insiders and outsiders. Nor does continuing joint I/O work make sense when, once the research has begun, an insider places strict limits on the types of issues that can be explored, limits that make it impossible for the research to address initially agreed-upon questions. Another problematic condition arises when a research project may well result in an exposé. In this case, it might be very difficult for an insider who does not want to be identified as a whistle-blower to be associated publicly with the study. The existence of too many relevant differences among possible members of a research team, such as in skills, interpersonal style, or lack of interpersonal competence, also suggests that the situation is not right for joint I/O work.

Ledford and Mohrman (1993) describe other situations in which I/O work may be impractical. In some cases, the setting being studied can remain anonymous if only outside researchers' names appear as authors; consequently, some organizations prefer that insider researchers not coauthor papers. Sometimes coauthorship by one of the setting members plays into difficult political dynamics in the setting, such as when some setting members view an insider author as taking undue credit through coauthorship. Ledford and Mohrman also observe that some statements about a setting could be made by academic researchers without penalty, whereas the same statements by an insider might politically jeopardize a career.

Conclusion

Particular challenges and ambiguities associated with social science research are heightened in I/O research. This is the case because in I/O research, boundaries between outside researchers and some research participants are reduced and because outside and inside researchers typically need to learn new ways of working with their counterparts. It is not possible to develop procedures that fully eliminate these ambiguities and tensions. Instead, our aim in this chapter has been to increase awareness of them and to increase awareness of occasions when an I/O approach is more or less feasible. We hope that this awareness will help researchers anticipate and deal more effectively with problems as they arise.

6. LESSONS FROM INSIDER/ OUTSIDER TEAM RESEARCH

As we conclude this monograph, two lessons associated with doing I/O work stand out as worth underscoring and elaborating. First, the contributions of I/O research come about as insiders' and outsiders' joint work creates a kind of marginal lens through which to examine subject matter. This lens is created by crossing experientially and cognitively different standpoints. It requires maintaining tension and distinctness among the standpoints. Second, the relational foundation on which joint I/O work rests represents a shift in the power dynamic that characterizes many forms of social science research. An appreciation of both these issues lies at the heart of doing I/O work well. Although we will discuss these points in more detail below, we first want to emphasize that each is as much a matter of practice as it is of perspective. When an outsider's or insider's espoused perspective differs from the perspective-in-practice (cf. Argyris & Schön, 1974), it will be discernable to the other party, and when only lip service is paid to needed power sharing, this disparity between practice and "press release" will be discerned in the story told. Each perspective must be reflected in one's way of being and in one's appreciation of the endeavor itself.

THE YIELD: THE VANTAGE
OF A MARGINAL PERSPECTIVE

The result of I/O research conducted well is the approximation of the uniquely insightful vantage of the marginal person. As Thorstein Veblen noted, "Marginality—the quality of being neither altogether inside or altogether outside the system—informs the intelligence and gives the marginal man [*sic*] the third eye that penetrates the culture as no insider could" (cited by Bennis in Handy, 1989, p. ix).

In insider/outsider pairings, the outsider's assumptions, language, and cognitive frames are made explicit in the insider's questions and vice-versa. The parties, in a colloquial sense, keep each other honest—or at least more conscious than a single party working alone may easily achieve.

Given that this knowledge yield arises as a marginal perspective is forged, it is critical, as we discussed in Chapter 5, that members of the team monitor and maintain the experiential and cognitive distance between themselves. It is in this tension that insights about how to conduct the inquiry and about the setting and phenomenon examined are generated. It is as a result of this tension that the greatest contribution of I/O teams occurs, regardless of whether the research has a more scholarly or more applied orientation.

THE FOUNDATION:
A FUNDAMENTAL POWER ISSUE

In calling for a new perspective on fieldwork, ethnomusicologist Judith Becker (1991, p. 394) strongly enunciates the need for a shift in power between outside academic fieldworkers and insider setting members.

> Learning to understand fieldwork as an extension of colonialism, as an instance of the inequalities of discourse, of ourselves as the possessors and controllers of the discourse about various "others," means a redefining of our whole discipline. For some it will mean giving up fieldwork entirely. For others, it will mean trying to find ways of doing fieldwork with a greater degree of reciprocality and reflexivity, using devices such as collaboration or dialogic writing. Sending a copy of one's book or dissertation "back" as was done in the seventies and eighties is scarcely anymore adequate.

In a similar indictment undertaken from a practitioner's perspective, Wing responds to the publication of the 1993 address by the president of the Academy of Management by giving "two cheers" for President Donald

Hambrick's assessment that the Academy of Management is irrelevant to the practice of management. Wing challenges the Academy of Management to "invite its research 'subjects' into its conferences and publications as equals," noting that "to date, those who wrote the papers had a monopoly on explanation . . . the test of truth was 'peer' review without practice" (1994, p. 388). Together, Wing and Becker signal that any inquiry into human systems needs to involve the human members of those systems as active participants in the inquiry rather than merely as passive subjects, respondents, informants, or practitioners. They signal a needed departure from what has been considered acceptable inquiry practice within and beyond the academy.

This shift in power is necessary if insiders and outsiders are to maintain a dynamic tension that enables a marginal lens to be applied. It is also core to another basic question: Do members of settings that are being studied have a right of ownership over the interpretation of their own experience? As symbolic interactionists have shown, people act on the basis of the meaning a situation has for them; an actor's definition of the situation is real in its consequences for that actor (Ball, 1972). Outside researchers often have acted as if they were the "possessors and controllers" of legitimate interpretations of a situation. Of what truth value are interpretations made without benefit of insiders' input or review (Louis, 1981)? As we have seen, outside researchers often are unable to understand insiders' experience.

An additional caveat with respect to the issue of power and control concerns a sometimes shallow understanding of what genuinely joint influence can mean. The situation is not unlike the contrast between participative management practices of the 1960s and some empowerment practices today (Louis, 1986). In the 1960s, supervisors were urged to invite subordinate participation in the design of various aspects of work processes; however, the impetus for participation and the subject matter on which input was solicited remained solely under the supervisor's control. When participation by either insider or outsider is controlled by the other party, only lip service is being paid to the notion of reciprocal influence over the conduct of a research project. This decreases the likelihood of creating a marginal perspective. Today, change agents and others speak of "empowerment," by which they mean fostering initiative and discretion on the part of the workforce. This differs from participation of old in that the timing, focus, and extent of an individual's initiatives are less at another's discretion. Such a shift parallels what is required for joint inquiry in which both insiders and outsiders have their own say, which, in turn, helps achieve the needed productive tension between them.

Enhancing Insider/Outsider Practice

The use of joint I/O inquiry is on the rise, whether or not it is labeled explicitly as such. This is evident in the number and variety of examples we have provided, especially from fields of study such as organizational behavior, community psychology, and educational research that are not grounded in a fieldwork tradition. The spread of inquiry in which those close to the phenomenon under study join with more detached parties who bring skills of systematic study has been fueled by and is evidenced by growing interest in participatory action research (e.g., Deshler & Ewert, 1995; Whyte et al., 1991), narrative inquiry and postmodern approaches (e.g., Boje, 1995; Clandinin & Connelly, 1994; Hassard & Parker, 1993), feminist approaches (Calás & Smircich, 1992; Oleson, 1994), and recognition of colonialist assumptions underlying traditional fieldwork practices (Becker, 1991; Diamond, 1990). Although the term "I/O team research" is not often applied to these forms of research, it accurately describes how the work is being conducted.

Becoming aware of commonalities among approaches to inquiry in terms of who the researchers are and how they work together can expand the pool of examples from which we can learn. It also may encourage researchers engaged in more applied work to learn from those who do more basic work, and vice versa. Whether the work is applied or basic, many aspects of the relationship between outsiders and insiders are similar.

Recognition of the extent to which a particular endeavor represents joint I/O research should be expanded. As we suggested in Chapter 1, there undoubtedly are many studies that are in fact joint I/O work but are not understood as such by their authors. Expanded use of the I/O concept can make its contributions, drawbacks, and dilemmas salient to researchers and increase outsiders' skill in both using it and describing it for others.

Much work remains to be accomplished if I/O inquiry is to be furthered. In this book, we have presented one mode of I/O joint work, oriented especially toward areas that do not have a fieldwork tradition. There are, no doubt, other models that may be more appropriate for areas in which such a tradition is established and in which outside researchers typically learn from informants. Here, as Becker (1991) suggests, the focus may need to be primarily on new types of relationships. It would be valuable to compare ways I/O work is being accomplished and has been accomplished in these different settings.

In addition, certain changes in common practices may be warranted. For example, the practice typical in writing up research is to feature the results of the inquiry and give sketchy information about the methods by which these results were generated, especially in terms of relationships and interactions among researchers that have had a significant impact on the course of the study. In the future, more needs to be said about the relationships among those involved in the study, through which the particular results were achieved (e.g., Dutton, Bartunek, & Gersick, 1996). It may be useful on occasion to have a forum in which the primary focus is on description of the joint process. Such forums might take shape as special issues of research journals or focused conference sessions. Perhaps if increased attention is paid to such issues, it will become a matter of course to attend to and report on how multiple perspectives are developed, maintained, and negotiated throughout a study. Until that time, however, it will be important to help one another attend to this aspect of inquiry, legitimize such a focus, and provide outlets for discussion about it.

Further, it is necessary to disseminate information about multiple forms of I/O collaboration. Having at hand a variety of templates can contribute to the quality of work as well as the efficiency with which it is done. Toward that end, we close by relating briefly what is being done in three studies in progress that extend outsiders' and insiders' roles beyond the examples we already have presented. Two of the three cases involve outside researchers from the United States working with insider setting members in other countries. In all three cases, the outside researchers served as resources, teachers, and coaches for the insiders who directed the inquiries.

In the first case, L. David Brown, a social scientist and participatory researcher affiliated with Boston University, worked over the course of a year with one national and eight regional nongovernmental organizations (NGOs) to carry out research on popular participation in development projects throughout the Indian subcontinent. The NGOs each worked with a different grassroots development project to assess the extent of grassroots participation in the project, the factors that helped or hindered participation, and the consequences of such participation. The outsider's role was to provide four week-long seminars over the year through which the NGOs learned research skills (including case writing, data gathering, data analysis, and interpretation of results), looked in depth at their own development projects, generated substantive learnings relevant to practice across those projects, and generated documentation of the inquiry process. The outsider was charged as well with preparing a manual for use by these and other NGOs to document the research methods and the training process by which team members worked together (Brown, personal communication, October 6, 1994).

In a parallel manner, Molly Lynn Watt and Daniel Lynn Watt, directors of the LOGO action research collaborative at the Educational Development Center, have developed a training program that prepares cohorts of "teacher-leaders" to facilitate groups of teachers in conducting teacher-research on their own classroom practices (Molly Lynn Watt, personal communication, July 14, 1995; Watt et al., in press). Facilitators-in-training learn about modes of inquiry, action research, and processes for facilitating meetings of the group of teachers with whom they will work throughout a school year. Facilitators create a network—electronic and personal—among themselves and with the directors to support teachers through phases of observation and research practice, question formulation and data gathering, data analysis, reporting, and presentation. Members of the teacher groups work together under the guidance of the teacher facilitator to identify a personally significant issue on which to focus within a larger domain of common inquiry selected by the group (e.g., teaching mathematics). Teachers serve as sounding boards and resources for one another through the process of designing, conducting, and reporting on their inquiry. Along the way, participating teachers and teacher-facilitators serve "as co-researchers with the project directors to develop materials, approaches, and methodologies for use by leaders of other action research collaboratives" (Watt et al., in press). This type of work serves teachers across multiple settings and makes them less reliant on outside researchers as sources of knowledge.

In the final case, Carlota Duarte (1994; personal communication, October 25, 1994), a visual artist and photographer, has been working with members of several Mayan communities in Chiapas, Mexico, to teach them technical aspects of photography, camera use, and darkroom practice. She specifically does not pass on guidelines for composition, framing, or other aesthetic aspects of photography. As a result, choices about themes of projects as well as expository processes are left strictly up to the insiders. The outsider provides only technical assistance.

The results are photo essays that document and represent native beliefs and use photographic images in ways very different from those of Westerners. Cultural preservation and creativity are key to the project. One reviewer (Bellinghausen, 1994, p. 13) noted that the people participating in the project (the Tzotiel) "are [now] able to be gatherers, not only the seen and looked at, but themselves the contemplators, generators of images in their own terms."

These examples expand our understandings of the ways insiders and outsiders can collaborate and the benefits of their doing so. They expand the notions of who may be taught to conduct research and what methods of data collection may contribute to enhanced understanding. They suggest that a researcher's role may overlap with a teaching role, one that enhances the competence of insiders as inquirers.

Some Parting Words

We have begun other chapters of this book with quotations or stories that were pertinent to the subject matter addressed in the chapter. We will close with another. In an article questioning how "native" native anthropologists truly are, Narayan (1993) stated that carefully separating out

> who is an insider and who is an outsider is secondary to the need for dismantling objective distance to acknowledge our shared presence in the cultural worlds that we describe. . . . Given the multiplex nature of identity there will be certain facets of self that join us up with the people we study, others that emphasize our distance. . . . To acknowledge such shifts in relationships rather than present them as purely distant or purely close is to enrich the textures of our texts so they more closely approximate the complexity of lived interaction. (p. 680)

As we have tried to indicate here, no one is simply or solely an "insider" or "outsider" in any particular inquiry situation. At the core of I/O work is a concern for sensitively and respectfully appreciating this about ourselves and about one another. The challenge is to conduct inquiry grounded in this awareness—to carry out the task of inquiry professionally as social actors in personally relevant situations inquiring together with others. In our own work, we have found that in having a partner in inquiry, one whose interests and characteristics differ from our own, we are better able to help one another be faithful to these principles of inquiry.

REFERENCES

Adler, P. A., & Adler, A. (1987). *Membership roles in field research.* Newbury Park, CA: Sage.

Argyris, C., Putnam, R., & Smith, D. M. (1985). *Action science.* San Francisco: Jossey-Bass.

Argyris, C., & Schön, D. A. (1974). *Theory in practice: Increasing professional effectiveness.* San Francisco: Jossey-Bass.

Ball, D. (1972). "The definition of the situation:" Some theoretical and methodological consequences of taking W. I. Thomas seriously. *Journal for the Theory of Social Behavior, 3,* 61-82.

Barley, S., Meyer, G., & Gash, D. (1988). Cultures of culture: Academics, practitioners, and the pragmatics of normative control. *Administrative Science Quarterly, 33,* 24-60.

Bartunek, J., Foster-Fishman, P., & Keys, C. B. (1996). Using collaborative advocacy to foster intergroup collaboration—a joint insider-outsider investigation. *Human Relations, 49*(6).

Bartunek, J. M., Galosy, J., Lacey, C. A., Lies, B., & Wood, D. R. (1991). Leadership succession in a group formed to empower its members. In A. M. Herd & W. P. Ferris (Eds.), *Proceedings of the Eastern Academy of Management* (pp. 252-255). Hartford, CT: Eastern Academy of Management.

Bartunek, J. M., & Lacey, C. A. (1993, May). *The roles of narrative in understanding work group dynamics associated with confronting alcoholism.* Paper presented at the Inquiries in Social Construction Conference, University of New Hampshire, Durham, NH.

Bartunek, J. M., Lacey, C. A., & Wood, D. R. (1992). Social cognition in organizational change: An insider-outsider approach. *Journal of Applied Behavioral Science, 28,* 204-223.

Becker, H. S. (1980). *Role and career problems of the Chicago public high school teacher.* New York: Arno.

Becker, J. (1991). A brief note on turtles, claptrap, and ethnomusicology. *Ethnomusicology, 35,* 393-396.

Bellinghausen, H. (1994). Caligrafía de las cosas. *Luna Córnea, 25*(5), 7-13.

Boje, D. M. (1995). Stories of the storytelling organization: A postmodern analysis of Disney as "*Tamara*-Land." *Academy of Management Journal, 38,* 997-1035.

Brown, L. D. (1985). People-centered development and participatory research. *Harvard Educational Review, 55,* 69-75.

Brown, L. D. (1993). Social change through collective reflection with Asian nongovernmental development organizations. *Human Relations, 46,* 249-274.

Brown, L. D., & Tandon, R. (1983). Ideology and political economy in inquiry: Action research and participatory research. *Journal of Applied Behavioral Science, 19,* 277-294.

Calás, M. B., & Smircich, L. (1992). Re-writing gender into organizational theorizing: Directions from feminist perspectives. In M. Reed & M. Hughes (Eds.), *Rethinking organization* (pp. 227-253). London: Sage.

Cancian, F. M., & Armstead, C. (1992). Participatory research. In E. F. Borgatta & M. Borgatta (Eds.), *Encyclopedia of sociology* (pp. 1427-1432). New York: Macmillan.

Chesler, M. A. (1991). Participatory action research with self-help groups: An alternative paradigm for inquiry and action. *American Journal of Community Psychology, 19,* 757-768.

Clandinin, D. J. (1989). Developing rhythm in teaching: The narrative study of a beginning teacher's personal practical knowledge of classrooms. *Curriculum Inquiry, 19,* 121-141.

Clandinin, D. J., & Connelly, F. M. (1994). Personal experience methods. In N. K. Denzin & Y. S. Lincoln (Eds.), *Handbook of qualitative research* (pp. 413-427). Thousand Oaks, CA: Sage.

Clandinin, D. J., Davies, A., Hogan, P., & Kennard, B. (1993). *Learning to teach, teaching to learn: Stories of collaboration in teacher education.* New York: Teachers College Press.

Clark, C. T., & Moss, P. A. (1995, April). *Researching with: Methodological, ethical, and epistemological implications of doing collaborative, change oriented research with students and teachers.* Paper presented at the meeting of the American Educational Research Association, San Francisco, CA.

Coch, L., & French, J. R. P. (1948). Overcoming resistance to change. *Human Relations, 1,* 512-532.

Cochran-Smith, M., & Lytle, S. L. (1993). *Inside/outside: Teacher research and knowledge.* New York: Teachers College Press.

Collier, J. (1945). United States Indian Administration as a laboratory of ethnic relations. *Social Research, 12,* 275-286.

Comstock, D. E., & Fox, R. (1993). Participatory research as critical theory: The North Bonneville, USA, experience. In P. Park, M. Brydon-Miller, B. Hall, & T. Jackson (Eds.), *Voices of change: Participatory research in the United States and Canada* (pp. 103-124). Toronto: OISE Press.

Connelly, F. M., & Clandinin, D. J. (1990). Stories of experience and narrative inquiry. *Educational Researcher, 19*(5), 2-14.

Costanza, A. J. (1991). Participatory action research: A view from the ACTWU. In W. F. Whyte (Ed.), *Participatory action research* (pp. 70-76). Newbury Park, CA: Sage.

Costello, K. (1994, May 26). ILR professor emeritus reflects on being a participant observer. *Cornell Chronicle,* p. 4.

Craddock, E., & Reid, M. (1993). Structure and struggle: Implementing a social model of a well woman clinic in Glasgow. *Social Science and Medicine, 19,* 35-45.

Deshler, D., & Ewert, M. (1995, May 9). Participatory action research: Traditions and major assumptions. Available e-mail: Subject: Re: Video and PRA. Message ID 02110200abd53092fa19@[132.236.243.34PARTALK list8@CORNELL.EDU

Diamond, J. (1990, Summer). There is no THEY there. **Musicworks*, 47,* 12-23.

Diamond, J., & Polansky, L. (1994). *The new music commissioning project: Goals and problems in a cross-cultural music collaboration.* Unpublished manuscript, Dartmouth College.

Duarte, C. (1994, November). Indigenous photography in Chiapas. Presentation at Adams House, Harvard University.

Dutton, J. E., Bartunek, J. M., & Gersick, C. J. G. (1996). Growing a personal, professional collaboration. In P. Frost & S. Taylor (Eds.), *Rhythms of an academic's life* (pp. 239-247). Thousand Oaks, CA: Sage.

Dyer, W. G. (1987). *Team building: Issues and alternatives* (2nd ed.). Reading, MA: Addison-Wesley.

Elden, M. (1983). Democratization and participative research in developing local theory. *Journal of Occupational Behaviour, 4,* 21-33.

Elden, M., & Chisholm, R. (1993). Emerging varieties of action research: Introduction to the special issue. *Human Relations, 46,* 121-142.

Elden, M., & Levin, M. (1991). Cogenerative learning: Bringing participation into action research. In W. F. Whyte (Ed.), *Participatory action research* (pp. 127-142). Newbury Park, CA: Sage.

Ellis, C. J. (1994). Powerful songs: Their placement in Aboriginal thought. *The World of Music, 36,* 2-20.

Engelstad, P. H., & Gustavsen, B. (1993). Swedish network development for implementing national work reform strategy. *Human Relations, 46,* 219-248.

Evans, C. L., Stubbs, M. L., Frechette, P., Neely, C., & Warner, J. (1987). *Educational practitioners: Silent voices in the building of educational theory* (Working Paper No. 170). Wellesley, MA: Wellesley College Center for Research on Women.

Evered, R., & Louis, M. R. (1981). Alternative perspectives in the organizational sciences: "Inquiry from the inside" and "inquiry from the outside." *Academy of Management Review, 6,* 385-395.

Farmbry, D. R. (1993). The warriors, the worrier, and the word. In M. Cochran-Smith & S. Lytle (Eds.), *Inside/outside: Teacher research and knowledge* (pp. 272-276). New York: Teachers College Press.

Farrell, E. (1994). *Self and school success: Voices and lore of inner city students.* Albany: State University of New York Press.

Farrell, E., Peguero, G., Lindsey, R., & White, R. (1988). Giving voice to high school students: Pressure and boredom, ya know what I'm sayin'? *American Educational Research Journal, 25,* 489-502.

Frost, P. J., Moore, L. F., Louis, M. R., Lundberg, C. C., & Martin, J. (1991). Context and choices in organizational research. In P. J. Frost, L. F. Moore, M. R. Louis, C. C. Lundberg, & J. Martin (Eds.), *Reframing organizational culture* (pp. 327-334). Newbury Park, CA: Sage.

Gephart, R. (1978). Status degradation in organizational succession: An ethnomethodological approach. *Administrative Science Quarterly, 23,* 553-580.

Gioia, D. A., Thomas, J. B., Clark, S. M., & Chittipeddi, K. (1994). Symbolism and strategic change in academia: The dynamics of sensemaking and influence. *Organization Science, 5,* 363-383.

Goswami, D., & Stillman, P. (1987). *Reclaiming the classroom: Teacher research as an agency for change.* Upper Montclair, NJ: Boynton/Cook.

Grumet, M. (1988). *Bitter milk: Women and teaching.* Amherst: University of Massachusetts Press.

Gubrium, J. (1988). *Analyzing field reality.* Newbury Park, CA: Sage.

Hackman, J. R. (Ed.). (1990). *Groups that work (and those that don't).* San Francisco: Jossey-Bass.

Hall, E. T. (1981). *Beyond culture.* Garden City, NY: Anchor.

Handy, C. (1989). *The age of unreason.* Boston: Harvard Business School Press.

Hassard, J., & Parker, M. (Eds.). (1993). *Postmodernism and organizations.* London: Sage.

Heider, F. (1958). *The psychology of interpersonal relations.* New York: John Wiley.

Heller, T. (1989). Conversion processes in leadership succession: A case study. *Journal of Applied Behavioral Science, 25,* 65-77.

72

Hermans, H. J. M. (1992). The person as an active participant in psychological research. *American Behavioral Scientist, 36,* 102-113.

Howe, K. R., & Dougherty, K. C. (1993). Ethics, institutional review boards, and the changing face of educational research. *Educational Researcher, 22*(9), 16-21.

Humphries, M., Krim, R. M., & Bartunek, J. M. (1995, May). *Organization development in the public sector: Changes in a political knowledge-based organization.* Paper presented at the Conference on Change in Knowledge-Based Organizations, University of Alberta, Edmonton, Alberta, Canada.

Israel, B. A., Schurman, S. J., & Hugentobler, M. K. (1992). Conducting action research: Relationships between organization members and researchers. *Journal of Applied Behavioral Science, 28,* 74-101.

Kahn, R. L. (1986). Comments on Kelly. *American Journal of Community Psychology, 14,* 591-594.

Kelley, H. H. (1992). Common-sense psychology and scientific psychology. *Annual Review of Psychology, 43,* 1-23.

Kelly, J. G. (1986). Context and process: An ecological view of the interdependence of practice and research. *American Journal of Community Psychology, 14,* 581-589.

Kelly, J. G. (1993, August). *Ecological inquiry and a collaborative enterprise: A commentary on "The Chicago Experience."* Paper presented at the meeting of the American Psychological Association, Washington, DC.

Kelly, J. G. (1994). 'Tain't what you do, it's the way that you do it: Take two. *The Community Psychologist, 28*(1), 29-31.

Kelly, J. G., Azelton, L. S., Burzette, R. G., & Mock, L. O. (1994). Creating social settings for diversity: An ecological thesis. In E. J. Trickett, R. J. Watts, & D. Birman (Eds.), *Human diversity: Perspectives on people in context* (pp. 424-451). San Francisco: Jossey-Bass.

Kingry-Westergaard, C., & Kelly, J. G. (1990). A contextualist epistemology for ecological research. In P. Tolan, C. Keys, F. Chertok, & L. Jason (Eds.), *Researching community psychology: Issues of theory and methods* (pp. 23-31). Washington, DC: American Psychological Association.

Lacey, C. A. (1991). *Epiphanies of the ordinary: Narrative analysis and the study of teaching.* Unpublished doctoral dissertation, Harvard University Graduate School of Education.

Lacey, C. A. (1995, June). Panelist. In P. Foster-Fishman (Chair), *Creating empowering settings.* Panel conducted at the meeting of the Society for Community Research and Action, Chicago.

Lacey, C. A., Wood, D. R., & Bartunek, J. M. (1990, April). *A committee of teachers for teachers: The first year.* Paper presented at the meeting of the American Educational Research Association, Boston.

Lampton, A., & Tunstill, G. (1994). Aboriginal music students' views on Aboriginal music research. *The World of Music, 36,* 21-40.

Lather, P. (1988). Feminist perspectives on empowering research methodologies. *Women's Studies International Forum, 11,* 569-581.

Lazes, P., & Costanza, T. (1984, July). *Xerox cuts costs without layoffs through union-management collaboration* (Labor-management cooperation brief). Washington, DC: Department of Labor.

Ledford, G. E., & Mohrman, S. A. (1993). Looking backward and forward at action research. *Human Relations, 46,* 1349-1365.

73

Levin, M. (1993). Creating networks for rural economic development in Norway. *Human Relations, 46,* 193-218.

Levin, M. (1993). Creating networks for rural economic development in Norway. *Human Relations, 46,* 193-218.

Lewin, K. (1946). Action research and minority problems. *Journal of Social Issues, 2,* 34-36.

Lortie, D. (1975). *Schoolteacher.* Chicago: University of Chicago Press.

Louis, M. R. (1980). Surprise and sense making: What newcomers experience in entering unfamiliar organizational settings. *Administrative Science Quarterly, 25,* 226-251.

Louis, M. R. (1981). A cultural perspective on organizations: The need for and consequences of viewing organizations as culture-bearing milieux. *Human Systems Management, 2,* 246-258.

Louis, M. R. (1986). Putting executive action in context. In S. Srivastva (Ed.), *The functioning of executive power* (pp. 111-131). San Francisco: Jossey-Bass.

Louis, M. R. (1990). Newcomers as lay ethnographers: Acculturation during organizational socialization. In B. Schneider (Ed.), *Organizational climate and culture* (pp. 85-129). San Francisco: Jossey-Bass.

Louis, M. R., & Bartunek, J. M. (1992). Insider/outsider research teams: Collaboration across diverse perspectives. *Journal of Management Inquiry, 1,* 101-110.

Lynd, M. (1992). Creating knowledge through theater: A case study with developmentally disabled adults. *American Sociologist, 23*(4), 100-115.

Merrifield, J. (1993). Putting scientists in their place: Participatory research in environmental and occupational health. In P. Park, M. Brydon-Miller, B. Hall, & T. Jackson (Eds.), *Voices of change: Participatory research in the United States and Canada* (pp. 65-84). Toronto: OISE Press.

Merton, R. K. (1972). Insiders and outsiders: A chapter in the sociology of knowledge. *American Journal of Sociology, 78,* 9-47.

Mirvis, P. H., & Louis, M. R. (1985). Self-full research: Working through the self as instrument in organizational research. In D. N. Berg & K. K. Smith (Eds.), *Exploring clinical methods for social research* (pp. 229-246). Beverly Hills, CA: Sage.

Narayan, K. (1993). How native is a "native" anthropologist? *American Anthropologist, 95,* 671-686.

Noblit, G. W. (1988). *Meta-ethnography: Synthesizing qualitative studies.* Newbury Park, CA: Sage.

Noblit, G. W., & Pink, W. T. (Eds.). (1987). *Schooling in social context.* Norwood, NJ: Ablex.

Northcraft, G. B., & Neale, M. A. (1993). Negotiating successful research collaboration. In J. K. Murnighan (Ed.), *Social psychology in organizations: Advances in theory and research* (pp. 204-224). Englewood Cliffs, NJ: Prentice Hall.

Nyden, P., & Wiewel, W. (1992). Collaborative research: Harnessing the tensions between researcher and practitioner. *American Sociologist, 23,* 43-55.

Oleson, V. (1994). Feminisms and models of qualitative research. In E. G. Guba & Y. S. Lincoln (Eds.), *Handbook of qualitative research* (pp. 158-174). Thousand Oaks, CA: Sage.

Pace, L. A., & Argona, D. R. (1991). Participatory action research: A view from Xerox. In W. F. Whyte (Ed.), *Participatory action research* (pp. 56-69). Newbury Park, CA: Sage.

Park, P., Brydon-Miller, M., Hall, B., & Jackson, T. (1993). *Voices of change: Participatory research in the United States and Canada.* Toronto: OISE Press.

Pasmore, W., & Friedlander, F. (1982). An action research program for increasing employee involvement in problem solving. *Administrative Science Quarterly, 27,* 343-362.

74

Rapoport, R. N. (1970). Three dilemmas in action research. *Human Relations, 23,* 488-513.

Reinharz, S. (1992). *Feminist methods in social research.* New York: Oxford University Press.

Roethlisberger, F. J., & Dickson, W. J. (1939). *Management and the worker.* Cambridge, MA: Harvard University Press.

Ryan, R. L. (1994, June 3). A view of action research, with an illustration. Available e-mail: Subject: Just some AR thoughts. Message ID 6051954.PAA02306@postoffice.mail.cornell.eduARTALK List LRYAN@CALVIN.STEMNET.NF.CA

Schutz, A. (1964). The stranger: An essay in social psychology. In A. Brodersen (Ed.), *Collected papers II: Studies in social theory* (pp. 91-105). The Hague, The Netherlands: Nijhoff.

Schwartzman, H. (1993). *Ethnography in organizations.* Newbury Park, CA: Sage.

Sutton, R. I., & Louis, M. R. (1987). How selecting and socializing newcomers influences insiders. *Human Resource Management, 26,* 347-361.

Torbert, W. R. (1991). *The power of balance.* Newbury Park, CA: Sage.

Trist, E. L., & Bamforth, K. W. (1951). Some social and psychological consequences of the longwall method of coal-getting. *Human Relations, 4,* 1-38.

Van Maanen, J. (1988). *Tales of the field: On writing ethnography.* Chicago: University of Chicago Press.

Watt, M. L. (Ed.). (in press). *Action research and the reform of mathematics and science.* New York: Teachers College Press.

Watt, M. L., Watt, D. L., McKiernan, J., & Schwartz, E. (in press). The LOGO action research collaborative: A case study from four perspectives. In M. L. Watt (Ed.), *Action research and the reform of mathematics and science.* New York: Teachers College Press.

Weick, K. E. (1989). Theory construction as disciplined imagination. *Academy of Management Review, 14,* 516-531.

Whitmore, E. (1994). To tell the truth: Working with oppressed groups in participatory approaches to inquiry. In P. Reason (Ed.), *Participation in human inquiry* (pp. 82-98). London: Sage.

Whyte, W. F. (1982). Social inventions for solving human problems. *American Sociological Review, 47,* 1-13.

Whyte, W. F. (Ed.). (1991). *Participatory action research.* Newbury Park, CA: Sage.

Whyte, W. F. (1993). *Street corner society* (4th ed.). Chicago: University of Chicago Press.

Whyte, W. F. (1994). *Participant observer: An autobiography.* Ithaca, NY: ILR Press.

Whyte, W. F., Greenwood, D., & Lazes, P. (1991). Participatory action research: Through practice to science in social research. In W. F. Whyte (Ed.), *Participatory action research* (pp. 19-55). Newbury Park, CA: Sage.

Wing, K. T. (1994). Two cheers for the Academy. *Academy of Management Review, 19,* 388-389.

Wolcott, H. F. (1973). *The man in the principal's office: An ethnography.* New York: Holt, Rinehart & Winston.

Wolcott, H. F. (1990). *Writing up qualitative research.* Newbury Park, CA: Sage.

Wood, D. R., & Lacey, C. A. (1991). A tale of teachers. *NWSA Journal, 3,* 414-421.

Worthy, J. C. (1993). From practice to theory: Odyssey of a manager. In A. Bedeian (Ed.), *Management laureates: A collection of autobiographical essays* (Vol. 3, pp. 375-414). Greenwich, CT: JAI.

ABOUT THE AUTHORS

JEAN M. BARTUNEK is Professor of Organizational Studies in the Carroll School of Management at Boston College. Her Ph.D. in social and organizational psychology is from the University of Illinois at Chicago, and she was a visiting assistant professor in the Organizational Behavior group at the University of Illinois at Urbana-Champaign. She has published more than 50 journal articles and book chapters, coauthored *Creating Alternative Realities at Work* with Michael Moch (1990), and coedited *Hidden Conflict in Organizations* with Deborah Kolb (1992). Her primary substantive research interests are in intersections of organizational change, conflict, and social cognition, especially with regard to how multiple cognitions affect the course of change. She has been conducting joint insider/outsider studies for several years.

MERYL REIS LOUIS is Associate Professor of Organizational Behavior at the School of Management at Boston University, where she also was a senior research associate at the Center for Applied Social Science for 5 years. Before returning to UCLA for her Ph.D. in the organizational sciences, she served on the consulting staff of Arthur Andersen & Co. and worked as a paraprofessional counselor at a community mental health center. Her substantive research has focused on career transitions and organizational socialization, workplace cultures, and cognitive processes in organizational settings. She has been an active participant in the discourse on epistemology and methodology in the organizational sciences and is the coeditor of two books on organizational culture.

Qualitative Research Methods

Series Editor
JOHN VAN MAANEN
Massachusetts Institute of Technology

Associate Editors:
Peter K. Manning, *Michigan State University*
& Marc L. Miller, *University of Washington*

Other volumes in this series listed on outside back cover